✫

THE
NBC
BOOK OF
STARS

✫

EARL WILSON

✫

CARICATURES BY
WACHSTETER

✫

POCKET BOOKS, INC. • NEW YORK

THE NBC* BOOK OF STARS

POCKET BOOK edition published December, 1957
1st printing .... October, 1957

*"NBC" is a registered trade and service mark
of the National Broadcasting Company, Inc.

H

"TODAY EVERYBODY IS CANDID,"

says Earl Wilson, famed Broadway columnist. "Sometimes they even floor me with
their answers — and I don't blush easily."

In **THE NBC BOOK OF STARS,**

the frankness that has won Wilson thirty million readers
gives you a unique and personalized introduction to your
favorite TV stars.

Here is the first really fresh and intimate close-up of the
celebrities everyone wants to know the truth about:

STEVE ALLEN • PERRY COMO

EDDIE FISHER • GROUCHO MARX

DAVE GARROWAY • GEORGE GOBEL

BOB HOPE • MILTON BERLE

TENNESSEE ERNIE FORD

DINAH SHORE • GISELE MacKENZIE

ARLENE FRANCIS

And caricatures of the stars by Wachsteter, too.

CONTENTS

THE NBC BOOK
OF STARS

ERNIE FORD'S

VITAL STATISTICS:

Born, Fordtown, Tenn., February 13, 1919; worked on folks' farm in Bristol, Tennessee, until age fifteen.

Enjoys hunting, with emphasis on possum and raccoon. Worked in dry-cleaning plant and as a grocery clerk before becoming an announcer at Bristol radio station.

Studied voice privately until 1939, when he was enrolled at the Cincinnati Conservatory of Music. First called himself Tennessee Ernie on station KXLA Western disc-jockey show. This program was his springboard to stardom.

Played London Palladium, April, 1953.

Wife, Betty. Two sons Jeffrey Buckner, age seven, and Brion Leonard, age five.

Capitol recording, "Sixteen Tons," sold over three million records.

During World II was a navigator, U.S. Army Air Force.

COUNTRY (MUSIC) BOY MAKES GOOD

Tennessee Ernie Ford, the cute, mustached, six-foot, pipe-sucking, pea-picking Plato of the country-music field, told me in simple language not long ago how to get into TV's Top Ten.

3

"You have to be somebody they can watch sittin' there in their pajama tops," he said, as he puffed on his briar.

"You can't be the kind of a guy they got to get up and put their clothes on for."

We were having lunch in Mike Lyman's restaurant in Hollywood. Ernie was so busy that he had just forty minutes to down his lunch.

"I'd like to hear you elaborate a little on that theory," I said.

Ernie had on an open-throated sports shirt. I kept thinking that all the women thought of him as handsome. He's outdoorsy-looking, and breezy, and a little homespun. But you can't call him just a rube or a hillbilly, for he spent a few months at the Cincinnati Conservatory of Music trying to learn how to be a concert singer. The very sophisticated Mortimer Hall, an old friend of mine, who owns a Los Angeles radio station and is married to the attractive actress Diana Lynn, came over and greeted Ernie warmly.

The kid from a wide place in the road known as Fordtown, Tenn., had clearly made it very big.

"Well," he explained, "I like to be watched or listened to not because of my talent—and I know I don't have too much— but because people like to have me around."

I waited for him to go on. "It's the same as a bunch of guys will call you to go fishin' every year because they don't have to dress up and put on airs. It's like that on TV. When you're in their home you can't get any closer to them, so you have to be the kind of a guy that's welcome there."

So it would appear that Tennessee Ernie's popular partly because he works at being a nice guy.

He has his chances to be smart-alecky and witty and flip, but he'd rather be pleasant, even though he does get off lots of Tennessee Ernieisms.

His simple background helps him be "just folks."

"This Fordtown, Tenn., that you came from—was that named for your family?" I asked him.

"Well, yes, the Fords used to live in that part of the country. They were poor people. My dad just retired after thirty-seven years with the post office in Bristol. He carried for seventeen years and worked inside for twenty years."

"I think I met you the first time at the Copacabana in New York," I said.

"Yes, that was in '52."

"Who was the star of that show?"

"Carmen Miranda. I was the extra added attraction."

"I'm curious about you going to the Conservatory of Music in Cincinnati," I said.

"My folks had aspirations that I would someday be on the stage," he told me. "I worked on the local radio station as an announcer, $10 a week.

"In high school I did Gilbert and Sullivan operettas. Naturally, your folks are enthusiastic. They thought of me growing up and doing concert work or something.

"In 1939 I entered Cincinnati Conservatory to major in voice. I had just a little bit of money, and I sang in my instructor's church choir to make a little bit more.

"I went home at Thanksgiving. Things were real rough at home. The folks were havin' a real bad time. I felt that my not working made it harder on them and I'd better go to work and help buy some coal for the winter. It would take some strain off of them.

"I had my bags packed to go back to school.

"Just then I got a call from station WATL in Atlanta, offering me a job as an announcer."

"As a disc jockey?" I asked.

"No. Just staffin'. So I took my bags and went south instead of north."

Ernie enlisted in the Air Corps when World War II began, was stationed in California, and married Betty Hemminger Sept. 18, 1942, in San Bernardino. After he was discharged from the Air Corps, Ernie had sort of given up radio and was thinking about going back to farming like his ancestors.

"Betty and I sat down and did a lot of figgerin'," he told me.

"We were both real serious about going up to the Yukon homesteadin'.

"You had to work for five years, and then you got the land that you staked out."

Again something happened to keep him in radio.

5

"I was offered a job on a local station, and so we took it and let it go at that," he says.

Maybe the fact that the third-handed car they were going to the Yukon in had broken down also influenced Ernie in his decision.

In San Bernardino, Ernie met a man who was to shape his life—Cliffie Stone, a veteran of country-music broadcasting. He had a weekly program, "Hometown Jamboree," Ernie began singing on it, and he got invited to do guest shots on other shows, and began making recordings. Cliffie Stone became Ernie's personal manager.

He still is his manager, and "As far as I know," says Ernie, "Cliff and I will be together for quite some time."

Ernie was in his early thirties before he really got discovered—but he moved pretty fast as soon as he got started.

People liked him immediately. They liked his Tennessee manner, although he never overdid it.

"At first when I was disc jockeyin', I would sing along with the records, same as on any disc-jockey show," he says.

"But I wasn't tryin' to cram my state down anybody's throat, because I don't think you can. But it seems to me that a lot of common ordinary conversation where I come from seems very funny to some people."

Three big records rocketed him to national attention.

"Mule Train" was first, then came "Shotgun Boogie" in '51.

"After 'Mule Train,'" says Ernie, "a lot of things started happenin'. I recorded 'I'll Never Be Free' with Kay Starr and that opened some doors. I began working such places as the Copacabana and Las Vegas. I was in the country-music field till then."

He had a Capitol Records contract, and it came time to make another recording.

"You got anythin' kinda different?" Cliffie Stone asked him.

"I said, 'Yeah'—just like that," Ernie remembered.

The "kinda different" song he remembered was "Sixteen Tons," written in 1947 by his friend Merle Travis and never able to get off the ground.

After Ernie recorded it, you could hear very little else for weeks.

"I liked it but even I didn't think anything like that would happen," says Ernie.

When we discussed it, it was heading for the 3,500,000 mark.

The record-pressers worked around the clock to turn out a million discs in the first three weeks. Many people not familiar with popular music began hearing the name of Tennessee Ernie for the first time.

He had sung this song about coal mining with such feeling that many listeners assumed he was from a mining family.

They learned that Ernie'd really done his first singing in jail in Bristol, Tenn.

The sheriff would have Ernie and his mother down to the lockup to sing hymns to the prisoners . . . a real "captive audience."

Maybe you don't remember the lyrics that everybody seemed to know so thoroughly in 1955:

"You load sixteen tons, what do you get?
Another day older and deeper in debt.
Saint Peter, don't you call me, 'cause I can't go.
I owe my soul to the company sto'."

Merle Travis was more a Kentucky singer than a Tennessee singer. He had made a folk-song album for Capitol in 1947, but nothing much had happened to it. There was no doubt about it that Ernie Ford's normally comic voice was this time "as mean as a blacksnake whip," as columnist Murray Kempton called it, when he sang:

"Some people say a man is made out of mud
A poor man's made out of muscle and blood
Muscle and blood and skin and bones
A mind that's weak and a back that's strong. . . ."

It was around this time that Lucille Ball and Desi Arnaz

7

established before the whole country that Tennessee Ernie was also quite a comedian.

Playing a country cousin in an "I Love Lucy" show—in which he didn't even sing one song—he was so funny that more new fields opened up.

"Jess Oppenheimer was doing the 'Lucy' show then," Ernie told me—mentioning one of the top TV creators. "He heard me doing a disc-jockey show and evidently felt I had some comedy possibilities.

"It was a great piece of writing—it was so funny," Ernie says.

Ernie was lucky in that the first script was evidently better than a subsequent one. Because if the first one hadn't been good, there might not have been another one, and there might not be a big Tennessee Ernie cult today.

All this took Ernie out of the country-music classification and made him a big citizen.

Ernie'd been mostly on radio and records, with just an occasional fling at TV. Then NBC-TV beckoned—and so did his old home state.

Tennessee Ernie Ford Day was celebrated on May 29, 1955. A big to-do was held in his old home town. Ernie was then thirty-six and actually on the doorstep of the big things.

When the Ford Motor Company first thought of sponsoring Tennessee Ernie Ford on TV on a nighttime show, the immediate reaction was No.

It was too corny an idea, everybody thought. It was too obvious.

Having a man named Ford working for Ford seemed contrived. Would anybody believe Tennessee Ernie's name was really Ford? After all, most people who knew him thought of him as Tennessee Ernie. —Wouldn't these people think Ford had added this last name as a sales gimmick?

Somebody else said, "But if the guy's good, won't it help Ford? After all, it'll be easy for everybody to remember who's doing the Ford show—fellow named Ford!"

"Right," reasoned another thinker. "Every time anybody thinks of Ernie Ford, they'll think right away of a Ford car.

"Talk about sponsor identification! What could be better?"

this gentleman went on. "First they think of a Ford car, let's say . . . then that makes them think of Ernie Ford . . . and when they think of Ernie Ford, then they think of a Ford car again. It's a chain reaction, so now they think of Ernie Ford again . . . and that makes them think of a Ford car again . . . and then . . ."

"Never mind!" said one of his listeners. "I think I get the idea. Once you get to thinking of either Ford, you're never going to quit thinking about Ford again as long as you live."

"All to the advantage of Ford!" the thinker said.

And so Ford Motors introduced Ernie Ford as TV's newest nighttime TV personality on Oct. 4, 1956. Within three months the show had become enormously popular. Carol Channing, Nelson Eddy, Corinne Calvet, Greer Garson, Zsa Zsa Gabor, Spike Jones, Adolphe Menjou, and Spring Byington, among others, had appeared on it.

It was voted "the best musical show" on the air in a poll of television editors, critics, and columnists conducted by *Television Today* and *Motion Picture Daily* for *Fame* magazine.

It all happened that fast.

Some of Ernie's philosophy is a little akin to that of Will Rogers and Arthur Godfrey, neither of whom he ever met.

His expressions don't always express a philosophy but more often just an idea. "That'll really mildew the sheets," for example, means that it was quite something. "Pert as a cricket," "slick as a peeled onion," "hotter than a bucket of red ants," and "as nervous as a long-tailed cat in a room full of rockin' chairs" are more or less self-explanatory.

"Who pulled your chain?" Ernie may ask a guest star.

"You look like a sack full of door knobs," he may tell another one.

About a husband who's henpecked he might comment: "Somebody slipped a ring through his nose when he wasn't lookin'."

A few others:

"Colder than a beaver's belly."

"Thicker than fleas on a wet dog."

"Tough as a hog's nose."

"Contented as a swarm of June bugs in a barrel of mash."

After he's asked a guest a question, he may say, "I handed you the bucket, you might as well milk."

"You dropped a clod in the churn," "You done plowed up a snake," "I'm as tired as a two-pound hen that's laid a three-pound egg," "I'm as eager as an octopus at a milkin' contest," "You're as nervous as a frog on a freeway," and "He's such a gambler, he'd make book on box suppers" are a few others that have made Ernie understood by millions—and misunderstood by quite a few, also.

One of Ernie's hobbies today is farming.

But he doesn't like to be called a "gentleman farmer."

"All a gentleman farmer raises is his hat," claims Ernie.

For a while after he started getting famous, Ernie, Betty, and their two children, Jeffrey Buckner (Buck) and Brion Leonard, lived a somewhat rustic life out near Whittier. "But there was too much freeway" with all the traveling Ernie had to do, so they became city slickers and moved next door to Bob Hope in the Toluca Lake section of North Hollywood.

Betty did most of the decorating herself.

"She didn't go to any fancy-schmancy Beverly Hills decorator with imported ideas," explains a friend. "She went to Barker Brothers, a local furniture store.

"The result is about what the average American would live in if they had a two-story ranch house . . . and were a little bit rich."

So you don't see Ernie out with the tractor much nowadays unless you happen to catch him back down in Bristol, where they had the big celebration for him, where he talked about red-eyed gravy with the best story-spinners in the county.

Red-eyed gravy's something you make from the leavings in the frying pan after you've country-fried some ham.

"You add a half a cup of coffee to your other ingredients," according to Ernie, "and then you eat it on everything, including the pie and the cake. Our family was pretty sloppy soppers. Of course we never had less'n three kinds of beans."

Ernie still likes to get Betty's folks to come over from San Bernardino, and Betty's sister to come down from San Francisco, so they can fling a family feast for fifteen or twenty with all the Tennessee-type fixin's he can round up in California.

At times like that Ernie'll get to reminiscing about his boyhood down in Tennessee.

He likes to remember the Saturday afternoons he worked in "Mr. Hughes's grocery store"—sweeping out, delivering, and best of all, "waiting on trade."

For twelve hours of work, he got one dollar.

One day while sweeping out, he knocked a dozen eggs to the floor. Eggs were about a quarter a dozen then.

Ernie saw one-fourth of his day's wages disappearing.

He remembers that he had a big temptation to sweep them off into the trash and not mention the mishap to Mr. Hughes. However, his Methodist upbringing, perhaps, took control, and he went to Mr. Hughes and told him of the calamity.

"I figure I owe you another three hours work," ventured young Ernie—not even considering now the possibility of giving up that dollar or any part of it.

The grocer congratulated Ernie on his honesty.

"So this time, we'll forget it." Mr. Hughes shrugged.

Ernie also enjoys recalling the summer days when he worked around the "threshing ring."

The farmers would go from one farm to another, threshing the oats, wheat, barley, and rye—and in their eagerness to get the threshing done while the weather was good and the grain was ripe, they would work as many as sixteen hours a day.

For sixteen hours a day, Ernie would get 50 cents.

But also he got his "board."

And what "board" it was! Each farmer's wife tried to outdo the other with the feast that she set before the threshers. Therefore each meal was a banquet.

On Christmas Eves, Ernie, his mother, father, brother Stanley, and the preacher would sing carols around town in an old truck—a coal truck which they borrowed from the coal man.

Sometimes they'd fill the truck bed up with straw and get most of the church choir to go along. They'd serenade the prisoners at the jails and then go on to the county poorhouse and the old ladies' home and the orphanage, taking along some Christmas presents—not that they had many to give.

As a kid, too, Ernie knew what it meant to go out into the cornfield in the dawn and pick off enough ears of corn to get the family some corn meal for supper that night.

He'd shuck it, shell it, sack it, and then climb aboard a mule and ride down past the church and the cemetery to the water-wheel mill.

The corn would be ground into meal, and then young Ernie would give the miller his share and take the rest home on the mule.

That night at the supper table they'd have the fresh crisp warm corn bread that came from the corn Ernie'd picked that morning.

When Ralph Edwards had Ernie on "This Is Your Life," Ralph wanted to re-create some of those days and undertook to fly Ernie's grandmother in from Bristol. This suggestion caused a sensation in Bristol, especially as his grandmother had never flown—nor did she ever intend to.

"I'm goin' up only once—and it ain't gonna be in an airplane!" she announced.

However, she gave in, and she loved it.

When success came in a big way to Ernie, he recognized its dangers.

He saw that unless he was on guard, his family life would slip away.

Therefore he determined that he would have to give up his very successful daytime TV show.

"If I don't, my kids are going to start calling me Tennessee Ernie instead of Daddy," he said.

"My daddy taught me to do so much!" he reflected. "Things that were a lot more valuable to me than winning an Emmy would ever be!

"So I want to spend some time with my kids, because pretty soon you're fifty years old and your kids have grown up and away from you."

Ernie had a big chance to make a motion picture—and a lot more money—this past summer, but he decided against it in favor of taking his family on the first tour they ever made of New England.

"Will you be driving?" I asked Ernie.

"Sure," he said.

I had my notebook out and was taking everything down dutifully.

"What kind of a car will you be driving?" I asked.

We both broke into laughter as we realized what a silly question I'd just asked.

GISELE MacKENZIE'S

VITAL STATISTICS:

Born Marie Marguerite Louise Gisele La Fleche, January 10, 1927; Winnipeg, Canada.

Marital status, single. Gave first violin recital at the age of twelve, Royal Alexander Hotel, Winnipeg. At age fourteen was admitted to Royal Conservatory of Music, Toronto, where she studied the violin for six years.

Vocal career started in summer '46, when bandleader Bob Shuttleworth employed her as violinist-pianist-vocalist.

In 1953 Jack Benny recommended her for solo spot on "Your Hit Parade." She got the job.

Height, five feet six; weight, 120 pounds.

Her mother, Marietta Manseau, was a concert singer and pianist.

Father—Dr. Georges MacKenzie La Fleche.

GISELE MAKES IT ALONE

Gisele MacKenzie has one of those startlingly fresh and friendly faces that actually make people stop and stare.

Come to think of it—although I say she has "one of those" such faces, I can't name anybody else who owns one. It is a very special face on a very special girl. Not long ago I dis-

15

covered how special her face was when we had a lunch date at the Hampshire House in New York.

I confess I was a little embarrassed at being in the presence of her good looks—also perhaps a little hurt that everybody noticed her so much and noticed me so little . . . let's face it, ignored me completely.

"After all," I tried to argue it out with myself, "I am known a *little bit* at least around that hotel. . . ."

But the headwaiter, the waiters, and the busboys bowed, drooled, and "Miss MacKenzied" her all over the place, and didn't seem to be aware of her celebrated escort (me) even being in the neighborhood.

What a blow it would be to the ego of any man who married her . . . and I wish hereby to give warning.

But allow me to describe a particularly enchanting example of the young woman's magnetism which unfolded there before my eyes.

It was quite undramatic and there is no punch line, no great dialogue. Let us say it is more an observation than a slice of reportage.

Gisele had brought along her two long-haired dachshunds and had hoped to stash them in the checkroom outside the pleasant dining room, one of the most "gracious" in New York.

But there was a customer ahead of her. He was an elderly, gray-haired, thinnish gentleman of obvious good breeding, the type who would carry an umbrella. Approaching the checkroom to claim his umbrella and perhaps his hat, he was doing very nicely—until he beheld Gisele.

He turned to stone.

He became deaf.

Still as a statue he stood, staring fixedly.

"Do you have your check, sir?" the woman attendant asked him impatiently.

She could be as impatient as she wished, for he didn't hear her. He continued drinking Gisele in, mouth slightly open.

"Your check, SIR?" The attendant was becoming—I hate to say it—curt.

Entranced, in the full meaning of the word, "in a trance,"

16

the fine old gentleman leaned somewhat forward but heard not. Shrugging bitterly, the lady attendant hastily grabbed hold of the dogs' leashes.

Gisele and I walked into the dining room. The old gentleman was still there, mouth slightly open, leaning forward a little like the Tower of Pisa.

Gisele the Bachelor Girl is unquestionably prettier and fresher-looking in person than on your screen. . . . . Startling Truth Number One.

And she is much prettier in her thirties than she was in her mid-twenties, when she was plump. . . . . Startling Truth Number Two.

Gisele looked, on this day I keep speaking of, as fresh as a girl who'd just won a Miss America title. She'd sloshed over in the rain to meet me, with the two dogs yipping along. Declining a cocktail, she ordered, as I recall, an herb omelet. With few preliminaries, I began talking to her about her bachelor-girl life—and the stardom that came along with it.

"I'll probably marry very late in life," she decided.

"Anyway," she added, "I think it's terrible how some mothers bring their daughters up to think that the main thing in life is to get a man.

"My mother"—and she smiled primly—"never did that!"

"So many mothers do," I suggested.

"My mother's attitude was, 'Don't worry about it.' What she wanted me to concentrate on was not men but the violin. I think she was quite right, too."

And then, in an unexpected surge of frankness, she exclaimed: "I'm a Catholic. That has a lot to do with it. I was about to take the plunge a couple of times and I didn't because of religion. I can see, looking back on it now, that it would have been the wrong thing to do!"

That we dropped as a touchy subject. What I wished to explore was how television had made a completely different person of Gisele.

Until she saw some kinescopes of herself around 1951, she didn't really know what she looked like.

"I realized," she told me, "I was fat!"

Never had this occurred to her before. "I was thirty-five

17

pounds heavier than I am now. I made up my mind, 'By golly, I'm going to get thin!' I went from size sixteen to size ten. I'm not much for exercise, so I took a year to lose it.

"Now I'm 122 pounds, and five feet six.

"My hair was long and parted on one side and down to the shoulders. I looked like a violinist—which I was!"

It was Jack Benny's admiration for Gisele that brought her along so fast. A girl of her talents would surely have attracted attention speedily elsewhere if Jack hadn't been around. Maybe it would have been a year or two later. Her talent must have been most obvious to the practiced eye, because when Jack "found" her he didn't even know she played the violin.

She was still a little bit plump in those days.

The first time I ever heard of her was from Jack. The first time that a lot of people ever heard of her was from Jack.

It was one noontime in 1953. Jack slid down at a table in the bar at Romanoff's. He was always eager to hear and dispense any show-business news of a constructive kind.

He exclaimed to us about this amazingly talented girl he'd seen working in Las Vegas.

"What'd you say her name was?" people like me would say.

"Gisele MacKenzie!" he'd say.

"Oh, yeah," we'd say, nodding blankly.

Gisele laughs a little about this experience. "I was there with Bob Crosby and the Modernaires playing the Sahara. I was what you call 'integrating' with the Mods [the Modernaires]. Mr. Benny came to see Bob Crosby, who was a regular on his program on radio and on TV."

Jack signed her up for his forthcoming tour, headed for San Francisco.

He still didn't know about the secret violin in her life. She had been trying to forget it—and now she had run into a man to whom little in life was quite so precious as his fiddle.

"I remember when we got to San Francisco," Gisele said, "my manager, Bob Shuttleworth, said, 'I think I'll tell him now you play the fiddle.'

"I didn't want him to. I wanted to keep it as a part of my dark, mysterious past.

"I'll never forget Mr. Benny's surprise. He said, 'Come over here, you little bum, and play for me! Why didn't you tell me you play the fiddle!'

"At the time I didn't even own a fiddle.

"He said, 'Now, you go out and buy a fiddle fast.' All our rehearsals on everything were brushed off that day while I went out and bought a fiddle."

Jack found out with a few questions that she really knew fiddling. She'd graduated in violin from the Royal Conservatory in Toronto. Jack always has said he "just picked it up" in vaudeville, and Phil Harris has always said, "You'd just better lay it down."

Jack was astonished that this girl half his age was so accomplished on his beloved instrument. "I practice all the time and she never practices," he moans, "but she plays twice as good as I do. It's not fair!"

Jack sought her advice eventually on violining.

"Do you think I ought to buy that new fiddle I saw today?" he would ask her, actually considerably worried about it.

"Oh, you've got a perfectly good fiddle," she'd tell him.

"Maybe this new one I was looking at would help me play better," he'd suggest.

She gave him no encouragement. "What I'm really looking for," he'd say, "is a fiddle that'll play itself." Shrugging, he'd say, "Maybe I'd better not buy it, then," and abandon hope.

Very early during Gisele's tenure with Jack's troupe she became a candidate for the singing job on "Your Hit Parade."

There were many other strong candidates. Jack discovered that Lucky Strike was considering Gisele as a possible replacement of singer June Valli.

"I think here might be an opportunity for me to help you," he said. "I'll put you on my television show as a guest singer and I'll show you off."

Gisele did so well, the whole country—including some of us whom Jack had told about her at Romanoff's—was talking of her talents the next morning.

"Two days later," she says, "I got the job."

Now Gisele was a big TV celebrity, singing the top songs of the nation every week. "Your Hit Parade" was a little opera troupe—everything was undertaken to dramatize the selection of popular songs that had to be sung—and it was wonderful experience for Gisele. But she wasn't happy.

No, she kept thinking of her own program.

Not "Your Hit Parade," but something simply explained, like the "Gisele MacKenzie Show."

It was three or four years off. Jack didn't quit helping her. When she was playing comedy and kidding around with some of the songs, she undoubtedly wondered how he'd play it.

"The songs got worse and worse for us and that became a harder test for us," she says.

"Rock 'n roll started to come in.

"At first there might be two or three of the top seven songs that we didn't like.

"Eventually it got to be seven out of the seven that we couldn't stand.

"But we had to do them anyway.

"People would say to me on the street or in the shops, 'I can't STAND those songs you sing now.' And I'd frankly say, 'I can't stand them, either.'"

However, they listened. Maybe they could stand them, after all.

Maybe Gisele and the others were making the songs more palatable than they realized.

They had some terrifying experiences.

"I was always horrified of television and still am," Gisele insists.

"Behind those two little red eyes on the cameras, there are millions of people.

"Well, I'm a nervous wreck after every show and swear I'm going to quit. Like, for example, sometimes you forget the lyrics. Well, you can't quit singing.

"So you make up something.

"Once I was doing 'That's Amore.' I had the pizza pie in the sky and the moon in the wine.

"Another time I had a scene with a horse.

20

"It was supposed to be a very romantic scene, nice and quiet and peaceful.

"And all the time the horse was clobbering me with its head and almost knocking me over!"

Gisele was getting good reviews in other efforts of a dramatic type. She starred in "Hard to Get," on NBC's "Justice" program, playing a singer who was cheated by her agent. In this show she introduced the song "Hard to Get," with a nineteen-piece orchestra behind her. The program was well reviewed and one month later it was repeated "by popular request"—something rather unusual and in its way a tribute to Gisele.

Still, though, people were saying, "Why don't you have your own program?" to Gisele La Fleche—that's her real name; she's the daughter of Dr. Georges MacKenzie La Fleche, a Canadian surgeon living in Winnipeg.

"They made me feel like I was in a rut. They kept yelling and screaming at me till I guess I felt a little hurt myself that I didn't have my own show."

And then one day Jack Benny said what everybody else was saying: "You've got to have your own show."

She herself wanted it but wasn't sure she was equipped.

"Too many people wait till after the boat has sailed," Jack said.

And thus in early 1957, J & M Productions, Jack Benny's company, began packaging the "Gisele MacKenzie Show" for NBC, with the help of Music Corporation of America, the big talent bookers.

Gisele at this very time was becoming an American citizen.

Her full name, which she got at birth, on January 10, 1927, is practically a sentence:

Marie Marguerite Louise Gisele La Fleche.

"I'm a French-Canadian and one-fifth Scotch," she says.

She didn't get started studying music very early—not until she was three. Her mother, Marietta Manseau, who had been a concert singer and pianist, started her on the piano when she was three. Her violin studies at the Royal Conservatory in Toronto continued for six years after her entrance there, and she won a scholarship in the Graduate School.

For musicianship, there's hardly anybody better trained in the popular field of television.

Getting her American citizenship was an overpowering emotional experience for Gisele—but she was also overwhelmed a little at the thought of leaving New York, which she had come to love very much, for California. She hated to leave the pink kitchen, with all its pink accessories, which she had collected herself and consequently adored.

"The pink kitchen was the hardest thing for her to give up," one of her friends told me.

For it was 100-per-cent pink—even the telephone, the frying pan, and the dish drainers. Some people thought she was a little hipped on pink—but Gisele, who at times looks remarkably like Nanette Fabray, and especially when she's trotting around the kitchen, always persuaded them that she wasn't daffy at all and that it all went along with her personality.

"It was the same about my bedroom," she declared at the time.

"I always wanted a lilac-and-white bedroom.

"But everybody said it wasn't done.

"Well"—and she laughed—"I done it, and I like it!"

One fine thing about the apartment on Central Park South was that it permitted the dachshunds, Wolfgang and Brunhilde von Bagel, to use Central Park for their strolls. It was also an excellent apartment to cook in. Gisele filled it with cookbooks and recipes, which her fans sent her by the score. She pasted them in scrapbooks.

"I'd rather read a cookbook than a detective story—and I love detective stories," she maintained.

It rather hurt her feelings that some people might think she was using cooking for publicity. Another facet of her character is her delight in mixing perfumes.

"There's no doubt about it, she's the sweetest-smelling doll on TV," one friend contended.

Comparing herself to some old witch mixing a brew, Gisele says she always stirs up her potions at night—and then never gets the same effect again. She forgets which perfumes she put into which batch. She doesn't know which witch she is.

One of her witch's brews she called "Mink."

"It was the color of mink, and when I smelled it, it reminded me of mink," she said.

Gisele, by the way, has a beautiful full-length mink—"given to me," she says, "with the compliments of Gisele MacKenzie."

Bachelor Gal Gisele made a stirring announcement when she met with the producers of her new show in March, 1957.

"Look, boys," she stated, "I'm a girl."

The assembled geniuses demonstrated that they didn't doubt this.

"I don't want to be bothered with a lot of details," she continued. "Leave that to the men who know how to handle it.

"Just give me the script and I'll learn my lines and come in and do them."

All this, of course, made a hit with the creative gentlemen on the show, who were so happy to hear that Gisele admitted she "doesn't know from all that and doesn't *want* to know from all that."

That was the one big reason Gisele had to move to California.

"Mr. Benny is going to be the adviser on the show," she explained. "And I can't imagine Mr. Benny advising by long-distance telephone."

"What kind of format are you going to have?" the press asked her at the beginning.

"Our format is more or less no format," Gisele answered. "Sort of along the lines of Mr. Benny's own show. The audience never knows what he's going to do the next time. Kind of loose, like."

But Mr. Benny made certain things clear, too.

He wouldn't appear on her first show.

She wouldn't play the fiddle on her first show.

She wouldn't play the piano on her first show.

She would, of course, sing on the first show.

"If he weren't advising," confessed Gisele, "I wouldn't be doing the show at all.

"I'd be just scared to death to think of it. But with his

23

knowledge and capacity, I think I've got a good chance. So I'm going to take a deep breath and take the plunge."

I mentioned that possibly she was the youngest girl to have her own show. She was just thirty.

"The only other one I can think of is Janis Paige," I said. The files showed Janis to be about four years older.

"How about Jeannie Carson?" Gisele asked quickly.

She was right. I looked it up. Miss Carson was just coming on twenty-nine at the time, about a year younger.

"How do you feel about the prospect of getting ulcers?" I asked her.

"I refuse to get ulcers!" she guaranteed me. "I think it is ridiculous. I'm not going to worry. I'll let the writers and the producers worry!"

"Are you the explosive type who gets everything out of her system?" I inquired.

"No. When I get mad, I clam up."

"Isn't that the ulcer type?"

"To me," she said, "a performer should have three things. Besides talent, of course, for I just assume a performer has some talent.

"Besides talent, a performer should have first, patience . . . second, a sense of humor and adventure . . . and third, a strong stomach."

"A strong stomach! I've never heard of that being a requirement," I said.

"I think I have all three. I love to cook—so I'd better have a strong stomach!" she laughed.

"What sports do you go in for?" I asked Gisele.

"Well, only summer sports, like swimming, because when I was a kid, I wasn't allowed to do sports," she answered.

"Why weren't you allowed to do sports as a kid?"

"I might break my arm—or develop the wrong kind of muscles—and then I couldn't play the violin!"

The fiddle has played such an important part in Gisele's life that the tale of "Fiddle Lost and Fiddle Regained" must be retold here.

Perhaps you've heard a little of this story. During World

War II, Gisele was twenty. She went off violining for the troops at some Canadian camps.

And she also sang.

"One of the navy boys" came over to her at one show and frankly told her she should quit playing the violin.

"Oh, I'm not so bad at it," she retorted.

"Dames that play violins don't make any money," the man said.

The "navy boy" was Lt. Robert Shuttleworth, leader of one of the Royal Canadian bands, and she listened to his advice.

Besides, it appeared that fate was on the same side. Somebody broke into her car and stole her very good fiddle.

After the war ended, Gisele heard of a job—singing and playing the piano for a resort orchestra.

While Gisele had never taken voice lessons, she'd practiced singing—and felt she could do band vocals.

So she investigated this job opportunity—and discovered that the band leader was the former lieutenant who had advised her to quit fiddling around.

Gisele went to work with this orchestra.

The leader subsequently quit the orchestra to become her personal manager, which he is today. He is, of course, the guy who told Jack Benny she could fiddle.

As for dames who can fiddle not making any money . . .

Gisele's good for around half a million a year.

"Do you have any fears about wearing yourself out on TV?" I asked her. "Of course," I pointed out, "you could have one of those five-year TV careers and retire a young woman at thirty-five."

"But the way taxes are, I can probably *never* retire," she said.

Anyway, she got from Jack Benny the conviction that it's the high-pressure performers who get ulcers and also get canceled and wear themselves out on TV. She contends that the low-pressure boys and gals don't disappear.

"I'm going to be so low pressure," she swears, "I'll hardly move."

GEORGE GOBEL'S

VITAL STATISTICS:

Born May 20, 1920, on northwest side of Chicago. Education, Cleveland Grade School and Roosevelt High School, where he met his wife, then Alice Humecki. Married, December 13, 1942. Three children, Gregg, born October 14, 1945; Georgia, born December 25, 1950; and Leslie, born March 30, 1954. Height, five feet five; weight, 138. Blue eyes, light-brown hair. Hobbies, golf, shoots in low eighties, usually plays with old Air Force buddies and cronies from early radio days. Also baseball and flying. Always carries guitar in car. Only child of Herman and Lilian Gobel. Favorite drink, Scotch.

GEORGE THE GREAT

George Gobel and I each have crew haircuts, and though I'm much older—and plumper—some people say there's a resemblance.

A few months ago, George gave a small party at the St. Regis in New York. Along with several other press people, I was invited.

It was necessary for me to continue on my news-gathering rounds. Therefore I stayed about twenty minutes, then said my farewell while other guests were still arriving.

I was leaving . . . was, in fact, about four steps from the door and striding toward it . . . when the door opened, and four more guests burst in.

An attractive Englishwoman I'd never seen before suddenly laughed, then lunged at me, grabbed my hand, seemed about to kiss me, and exclaimed, "Oh, Mr. Gobel, I've enjoyed you so much on television!"

George, off in a corner of the big room, shook his head and muttered, "I'll be a dirty bird."

Perhaps because of this resemblance, I've found out about the widespread female adoration for George. Occasionally I overhear women whisper "Isn't that George Gobel!"—always in great excitement. Grace Kelly and Nina Foch, in separate interviews I had with them, rhapsodized about Gobel. I asked Miss Foch, "Is it physical attraction . . . sex appeal . . . something like that?"

"No, it's just that he's so *nice*," she said. "You just can't imagine him ever hurting anybody."

Grace Kelly was quoting Gobelisms. One of her favorites was an exchange between George and Peggy King, when Peggy brought in a big sheep dog. Peggy that night was wearing a fox collar and a fox muff.

"What pretty furs," remarked George. "I see you had enough left over to make a dog."

Mitzi Gaynor, who played George's leading lady in their movie at Paramount, "The Birds and the Bees," was no less eulogistic. "She couldn't wait to come to work every morning because she liked working with George so much," one actor told me. When George came back from lunch one day, I noticed Mitzi rush up to him and—almost like a mother—say to the five-foot-five George, "Hiya, Hotsie.—What'd you have for lunch? Hot dogs, I'll bet."

"Hotsie" was his name in the picture; he was a hot-dog czar.

It can't be George's crewcut that's got all the women crazy about him. I know, because it hasn't happened to me. George and I did pose once for a picture showing us studying each other's crewcuts. His usual greeting to me now is, "Taken any more silly pictures lately?"

George—who called himself "Lonesome George" around the studio and even had that name on his bicycle—keeps his crewcut short all the time. A barber at NBC keeps it at the proper shortness. One day when George hadn't been around NBC for a couple of days, he reappeared, not looking very rugged.

"I've been sick," he explained.

"What was wrong?" they asked him.

"I've been in bed two days," he said, "with a terrible haircut."

It's George's word trickery—such as the sample above—that's been largely responsible for his sudden TV success, in my opinion. Gobel often outfunnies his writers.

Fortunately, George retains his breezy freshness, and his unexpectedness, even after surviving the early "wonder boy" hysteria about himself.

They were giving him a party at NBC's executive dining room in New York after arranging for him to star on alternate weeks in a team-up with Eddie Fisher.

"Where's spooky old Alice?" I asked George, using his own term for his wife.

"I put a chain on her and left her tied under the sink," he said.

George was concerned because the movie he made with Diana Dors, "I Married A Woman," had never been released by RKO which had curtailed operations so sharply that it was difficult to get an executive on the telephone.

"You phone out there," George told me, "and a watchman answers.

"That watchman was awful decent about it," George said, "and he was willing to release the picture any time I wanted to."

George is fairly careful, though, because of one of his early broadcasts, which he closed by saying, "It is not true that happiness cannot be bought. If you don't think so, stop off and buy a fifth on the way home."

Some temperance organizations still feel rather strongly about that.

I remember watching his company rehearsing a sketch about New Year's Eve. The theme of the show was that George wanted to go out partying and drinking. His wife,

Alice, wanted him to stay home, duck all parties, and not drink.

Midnight—the New Year—had come . . . the hour for hugging and kissing.

A man had dropped in to deliver a bundle, and George was to shake hands with him, and then he was to kiss his wife and wish her Happy New Year.

"Since she hasn't let me drink anything all evening, how about me shaking hands with Alice instead of kissing her?" spoke up George.

The idea of a sober husband saluting his teetotaling wife with a handshake instead of a sizzling smooch tickled producer-writer Hal Kanter, who called out to a secretary, "Put a gold star opposite George's name!"

It's doubtful if even Gobel completely appreciated the suddenness of his great fame. One July afternoon in 1954, I was in Reno to see Ava Gardner, who was at near-by Lake Tahoe preparing to divorce Frank Sinatra. I walked from the Hotel Riverside over to the Hotel Mapes and saw George Gobel wandering around the lobby.

He was headlining at the Mapes with his café act . . . yet I imagine I was one of two or three people in the lobby who would have found anything familiar about his name or his boyish face.

I knew him because I'd covered his act at the Waldorf. He'd been on TV a few times . . . but he was even then a comparative unknown.

In only about two months, he was the national rage and people were mouthing his "You can't hardly get them kind no more" all over the country.

Just a year later Gobel was making a movie in which he was the star, because of his great TV success.

It's doubtful if anybody ever came up so fast.

It was so fast, in fact, that when I mentioned to George how he'd been just a café performer one year before, he doubted it had been such a short time.

"It was longer ago than that, wasn't it?" he asked, seriously. "Wasn't it two years?" But it wasn't. His doubt made me doubt myself, and I got out my files. It all happened within a year.

Such a short time in which to become famous and wealthy . . . while still in the middle thirties!

The Gobel success story is the more amazing because he did it with an intellectual type of comedy that most comics would consider too dangerous to play around with—even if they understood it. He had demonstrated that there is an audience—and a vast one—for comedy that doesn't include seltzer bottles, baggy pants, and pratfalls.

Who but Gobel would have dared try to get a laugh out of a line about the Brontë sisters?

In one early script, his writers left him a note. The note said: "We've gone to lunch. Your writers, the Brontë sisters."

Gobel shook his head moodily upon reading this aloud.

"That's Charlotte's work," he decided sadly. "Emily would never have done that."

"Documentary comedy, that's what it is," George has said, continuing to kid himself about it. "We do drawling-room comedies."

Although I've been emphasizing the "suddennesss" of George's success, actually he'd been successful on the café circuit for several years—it was his TV fame that came dramatically quick.

The Gobels and their three children haven't done anything ostentatious about hitting the Big Money—as they were already doing all right.

George has resisted the Cadillac trend. He drives an Oldsmobile, and his wife has a Ford. Mrs. Lucy Humecki, George's mother-in-law, has lived with them almost since their marriage. Mrs. Gobel and her mother require no big staff—they do most of the housework, assisted by a maid or cleaning woman.

But there are always several guests around. For George seems unable to slough off even an accidental acquaintance from his days in Chicago.

When one phones, he's likely—if he gets through to George —not to be treated icily, but to be invited out to the Gobels' to stay a few days, and asked to bring the family. Or if he doesn't have a family, to bring somebody else's.

Consequently, there are people trooping through their three-bedroom, two-bathroom house in Sherman Oaks who are almost strangers to George. Literally hundreds of people in America consider themselves George's intimates because of this friendly attitude.

Word came back recently that one man said he and George were "inseparable."

George wasn't able to place him.

The Gobels' swimming pool often is being swum in by ten to fifteen children. Once recently, the Gobels had more guests than they could handle in their home and in their guest house.

They had to send two of their children out to stay with neighbors.

Of course, the movie made George more famous. One day I had a lunch date with him at the studio. He had reserved two tables—one for us, and one for some friends of Mrs. Gobel's who had dropped in.

"George'll be shuttling back and forth between the two tables," I was told. "He'll eat a little there and a little here."

Actually, it didn't work out that way. Some girl winners of a pretty-legs contest had arrived at the studio. They had to pose for pictures with George. That took about forty-five minutes, so "Lonesome George" must have had about ten minutes for lunch, and he justifiably gave eight of them to his wife and her friends, and two to us.

George took time to tell us a story about Jeff Donnell, who played his wife on the program. An autograph fan asked for her picture, and she signed it "Jeff Donnell."

As an afterthought, she added "Mrs. Aldo Ray."

After studying both signatures, the fan timidly inquired, "I wonder if you would also sign it 'Mrs. George Gobel'?"

She would and did.

The Gobel Success Story seems to have very few reverses, disappointments, or touches of tragedy in it.

And certainly no poverty, or sleeping on park benches, or going broke in Duluth.

Not once in his life has Gobel "had wrinkles in his belly" or "gone hungry."

His father, Herman Gobel, an Austrian, had a grocery and general-merchandise store on Chicago's northwest side. When George was a small boy, the family lived upstairs over the store.

Little Georgie Gobel waited on customers frequently enough to be able to impersonate them later.

When he was eleven, "Little Georgie Gobel, boy soprano," was on radio station WLS and has been working ever since. His voice changed, and it was time for him to get out of high school and into the war. He had met Alice Humecki at Roosevelt High, and they were married while he was in the Air Corps as a bomber pilot.

While he was a pilot, he was in a crash and suffered injuries that put him in a hospital. He came out and was made an instructor. At this time he had to make an important decision—whether to be a professional flier, a hillbilly singer on the radio, or a comedian.

For he had discovered while in the Air Corps that he could make people laugh.

He had been primarily a guitar player when he joined up. A commanding officer at his post in Oklahoma found that he could sing and invited him to the officers' club. They liked him there, and to give the singing some variety and the throat a rest, he tried telling a few jokes.

In short time, the C.O. was telling other C.O.'s at other posts that he had a fine young entertainer there, and that they should try him some night.

Gobel found himself being invited to fly hundreds of miles to put on a week-end show. He was fed well and pampered a little—and naturally, he liked it. He was still in uniform in 1946 when he went to the Chicago manager David O'Malley and told his story.

"I know you," O'Malley said. "You're a singer."

"Not now," Gobel answered. "Now I'm a comedian."

He asked O'Malley to look at him work, and to tell him

whether he thought he had any prospects as an entertainer.

"He wasn't especially funny-looking," O'Malley recalls. "He seemed to be a timid little fellow. He wasn't, but he gave you that impression."

A few nights later, O'Malley arranged for Gobel to appear at a big benefit in Chicago for the Armed Forces.

Gobel, although unknown, was a minor sensation.

He had his halting, apparently misdirected, undirected style of delivery even then. O'Malley promptly took him on and moved slowly with several steps that were a part of his gradual development.

Gobel discovered himself working in East Dubuque, Wichita, the Tower Theater in Kansas City, in Springfield, Ill.—in small cafés not heard of by people who don't live in those areas.

Finally George was ready for his home town—Chicago. He was booked into Helsing's, a vaudeville lounge, and became a fixture.

"He found people roaring at his stuff—and he probably didn't know why," O'Malley says. He gained confidence, and he experimented. Now he was ready to do his first hotel in the country—the Jefferson in St. Louis. Next stop, the Bismarck in Chicago. Each year he worked in better places; each year he made more money. He was not suddenly thrust into fame.

An interviewer asked his mother recently if it wasn't quite a shock to her for her son suddenly to become a big star.

"No," she said, "I had become conditioned to it. I could see it coming."

The Statler chain booked him—this was a huge moment—then he was booked into the Pierre in New York.

O'Malley reminded me that I was one of the two New York columnists who paid attention to him when he first arrived there.

I had to confess that I didn't especially remember him. That is the way it is with a young comedian.

When the press was invited to hear him in New York, the press generally would say, "George Gobel? Who is he? I never heard of him."

In my case, I happen to be a sucker for comedians. If it

had been the most sensational dancer who had come along in generations, I might well have said, "So what?"

Although he's fond of saying that he fell in love with Alice because she did his homework while he was out working on the radio, George is actually a very bright fellow. He finds this a good pose.

When people try to talk business to him, he often says, "I do the funny business and Mr. O. does the serious business. You had better talk to him."

Nowadays George is so busy that it's hard for even O'Malley to talk to him for any length of time. When O'Malley broaches a new venture for him, George often says, "I know you'll do the right thing, Mr. O."

That's been a guide for O'Malley. George has a substantial annuity program, an insurance program, a portfolio of stocks and bonds, and has invested in a group of motels in San Antonio, Phoenix, and El Paso, headed by Del Webb of the New York Yankees, who also built the Beverly Hilton.

"I don't like any kind of deals that are kinky," George sometimes says. O'Malley interprets this to mean anything off-color, shady, or under the table.

"I think George can be the Will Rogers of our era," O'Malley says affectionately.

While not religious—George's mother is an Episcopalian and he was once a choir boy—he has a quiet spiritual streak. Alice is a Catholic. Once, when O'Malley gave him a medal dedicated to St. Genesius, the patron saint of actors, the manager undertook to tell him its meaning. He was surprised to find that George knew more about it than he did.

MILTON BERLE'S

VITAL STATISTICS:

Born July 12, 1908, New York
City. Father, Moses Berlinger, a paint salesman;
mother, Sandra Glantz, a department-store detective. Fourth of five children. Three brothers, Philip,
Francis, and Jack; and younger sister, Rosalind. Education, completed eighth grade of Manhattan's Professional Children's School, mostly by correspond-
ence. Twice married to and divorced from Joyce
Matthews. Adopted daughter, Victoria (Vicki), born
1945. Married public-relations expert Ruth Cosgrove
December 9, 1953, New York. Doesn't drink. Smokes
eight-inch cigars. Hobbies, magic, billiards and playing benefits.

"MR. TELEVISION" BERLE

The night of Thursday, May 12, 1949, was probably the
happiest one in Milton Berle's life.

"Mr. Television" was the king that night of the comedy
world. About a thousand people, many of them famous, came
in black ties and evening gowns to the Waldorf to a $50-a-
plate dinner honoring "Uncle Miltie," who was receiving the
Interfaith in Action's award for furthering religious under-
standing. When the prominent dais-sitters settled down at
their places, each one found at his place a copy of the May
16 *Time* and the May 16 *Newsweek*. Each magazine had
Milton Berle's picture on the cover. So far as is known, the

coincidence of one man's face being on the cover of these two magazines the same week had occurred only twice before —the other men had been Winston Churchill and Franklin D. Roosevelt.

"The Child Wonder," sang out the headline on *Time*'s story.

"Television's Top," exclaimed *Newsweek*.

Berle truly deserved this applause, for he had made television almost as much as it had made him. His Tuesday-night show was receiving an 80, or better, Hooperating, meaning that four out of every five sets tuned in were dialed to Milton's clowning. Actually, the rating was probably even higher—very close to 100.

"Berlesday" was the nickname we gave Tuesday then.

Milton Berlinger was just forty and had been on TV only since the previous October. People said that Milton Berle had been responsible for selling practically all the 535,000 sets then in use in New York. People didn't buy TV sets to watch TV—they bought TV sets to watch Milton Berle. The remark that Berle was responsible for selling nearly all the sets became so commonplace that one comedian, Joe E. Lewis, a good friend of Berle's, kidded him about it. "Mr. Berle," Joe would say at the Copacabana, "has been responsible for the sale of millions of television sets; I know I sold mine, my brother sold his . . ."

This kind of jollity was to be expected because Berle had always been the master of the insult joke and, on stage, was the first to tear himself down and deprecate his material.

Even on that Thursday night in May, 1949, Berle did it. Somebody said in the course of a flowery tribute that he hoped Berle would live to be 102.

"I hope so, too," ad-libbed the guest of honor. "Then I'd be as old as my material!"

Milton's mother, Sandra Berle, a much beloved woman then nearing seventy-two, who has since died, was present at this gilded occasion, and Berle spoofed her as always. "How old are you, Mother?" he asked her.

"Fifty-nine," she answered, playing straight for her son, as she often did.

"Then how come I got a brother fifty?" Milton asked.

To round off the evening of praise for Milton's willingness and even eagerness to appear at benefits for worthy charities, the dinner committee presented a show headed by comedian Henny Youngman, Milton's long-time friend, with whom he playfully feuded on and off the air.

"I want you to know," Berle said that night, "that they have gone to practically no expense for this grand show."

The king was so much a king then, and so much time and so many television shows have passed since, that most of us have forgotten the importance of Uncle Milton to the wondrous medium.

It is only fair to look back a bit.

The *Time* magazine cover caption read, "Should he be investigated by the Atomic Energy Commission?" And then *Time* went on to word-paint the incredible situation existing toward eight o'clock Tuesday nights along the Eastern Seaboard in that magic year of Berle's career.

"Business falls off in many a night club, theater ticket sales are light, neighborhood-movie audiences thin," *Time* said. "Some late-hour shopkeepers post signs and close up for the night. In Manhattan, diners at Lindy's gulp their after-dinner coffee and call for their checks as they did in the days of the Roosevelt fireside chats. On big-city bar rails along the coast and in the Midwest, there is hardly room for another foot. . . ."

As one who lived through that Berle era, I'd say that *Time* even underestimated it. There'd been only one attraction up to then that could literally make people close up shop when it was on the air—and you had to go back to radio for that. Back to the early 1930's, when I saw Warden Preston Thomas of Ohio Penitentiary delay an execution for half an hour or so, that he might not miss "Amos 'n' Andy."

Berle had the advantage of being seen on a medium that was still crisply new and novel. He was justifiably cocky. He was, for one thing, a millionaire. CBS couldn't dredge up anybody who could make a dent in the ratings of Berle's "Texaco Star Theater," and it was no secret that CBS boss William Paley would have liked to steal Milton from NBC. Sid Stone, the pitchman, with his "Tell you what I'm gonna do" spiel, became a national celebrity just for his commercials, which, it should be pointed out, were amusing and entertaining even then. Later hucksters who like to claim that they thought of making commercials entertaining seem to have forgotten that Berle's show preceded them by several years.

King Milton put on his shows then in Studio 6-B at NBC, and a seat was a great prize. But for a reporter, the afternoon preceding the show, and the afternoon preceding that, afforded a fascinating study of a man who knew he was the top dog and was going to remain the top dog for a lot of years to come.

Berle's rehearsals were, in their way, the first "spectaculars" —Milton'd always be the generalissimo, wearing a towel around his neck like a fighter and blowing short, sharp blasts on a referee's whistle to herald some announcement or . . . sometimes . . . just to bawl out somebody for making too much noise.

The rehearsals became a Broadway institution, and all sorts of people managed to get in.

With a cigar in his kisser, Berle would show a chorus girl how to wiggle or explain to great tap dancer Bill Robinson how to deliver a joke.

"Nobody gives this fellow the credit he deserves," Robinson told me one afternoon at one of the rehearsals.

Berle's eyes—and ears—were on everything. While spouting camera instructions into a microphone, he would turn to the orchestra and ask, "What was *that* note? It didn't sound so good!"

And with his arm pistoning and a finger pointing, he would conduct the orchestra. Sometimes he would compose a song right there. He accomplished this by humming a "buh-buh-BUH-buh" melody to a pianist, who would write it down. The pianist would, in effect, be taking dictation.

When he had straightened out the orchestra and finished writing the song, Berle would return to the cast, which was rehearsing on camera.

But he wouldn't participate in the acting himself. For that he'd have a stand-in, usually his writer friend Hal Collins.

Sitting on a chair fifty feet away from the stage, he'd watch the performance over a TV set, blowing his whistle to quiet everybody so he could tell a guest star to punch a line harder or smile wider.

One afternoon I was at one of these rehearsals talking to Milton's manager, Irving Gray.

"Who's the head writer?" I asked Irving.

"Milton's head everything," he said. "If this guy ever gets sick, we're all on relief."

Henny Youngman was there that day making jokes. "Berle's so rich he lives at the Manufacturers Trust," he'd been saying. "If you want to see him after three, you have to go in through a chute. He doesn't hide his money under the rug. He puts his money on the rug and hides the rug."

There was some tittering around us, and suddenly Berle blew that whistle.

"Will you clear everyone out of the studio who's not in the cast?" Berle shouted.

Youngman and several others, including Milton's brother, Frank, slunk out somewhat sheepishly. Berle later called them back in, explaining he had meant some of the droppers-in who had no business being there.

Often Berle didn't know his own lines.

"Don't worry about me, I'll always think of something funny to say," he'd tell anybody who worried about it. Usually the rehearsals lasted until seven o'clock—an hour before the show began—and while he was getting made up, Berle would finish learning his own lines.

And then he'd go on stage before all those millions. . . .

It was fun being around the Berle of a dozen to fifteen years ago, because TV hadn't yet saddled him with responsibilities, and he was the "Perfect Fool," even more than Ed Wynn ever was.

Berle was trying for laughs every *second*.

"Berle only needs an audience of two, and one of them can be Berle," somebody remarked, accurately, at the time.

His eagerness to make you laugh at him was greater than his logic. As a young comic, he didn't mind being called the "Thief of Bad Gags"—it was at least a handle—but as he became famous, the tag grew irksome. One night in a night club he was explaining to me, seriously, for a split-second, that he wished he could shed the gag-thief reputation. As he discussed it, the master of ceremonies lured Milton to the microphone.

To my astonishment, Milton's first words were:

"I was listening to Jack Benny on the radio the other night and was he funny! I laughed so hard I almost dropped my paper and pencil!"

It was sure-fire and he knew it; he couldn't resist using it even though it helped perpetuate the thing he was fighting.

Actually, of course, Berle was stolen from by everybody else, too. Milton has never completely given up one of his lines, "You look like you've got my old nose"—but in the early forties, when he was in his early thirties, he got many a solid yak out of his confessions about obtaining a new proboscis.

"I went to a plastic surgeon—one of those guys that runs a clip joint for noses," he'd begin.

"My own nose was a pretty good nose as noses run, but now that I've got this, I'm going to Hollywood and do some nosereels. One girl I know told me I looked like Taylor. 'Sure,' I said, 'my tailor.' Anyway, I have a lot of fun on my own hook."

He found it hard to talk without using "one-liners."

"Just came back from Hollywood," he'd tell you, "and boy, did I make some pictures out there! Look at these snapshots. What a trip I had coming in! I kissed Betty Grable so much my face went right through the picture frame. We made one stop while I went to an Army camp. What a welcome I got. The whole regiment got down on their knees. Boy, did we have a crap game!"

His true story about his nose was less amusing than the above version. Back in 1932, while with Earl Carroll's "Vanities," he'd butted into a piece of scenery in the Brooklyn Majestic Theater.

A doctor called up from the audience patched up a split in his nose, but thereafter Milton had a big bump on it, and headaches . . . and a light in front of his eyes.

He got the nose straightened and the bump taken out and emerged quite good-looking.

"Boy, those were hectic days," he would relate. "And when I say hectic, I mean exciting, because I don't know what hectic means.

"My life's always been exciting. I once won a cup for imitating Charlie Chaplin. It was worth a dollar and was I proud! I used to take my relatives down to the pawnshop to see it."

This was the young, thirty-five-year-old Berle. He was then in the "Follies," as the star, and the richest young man in show business. Hopping into a cab after his performance, he'd spot the driver's name on the identification card . and immediately address him by his first name.

"Say, Dave," he'd say—if the driver's name was David Silverstein, as it happened to be one night—"take us to the Commodore."

That night, Enric Madriguera was opening there, and as Madriguera began sawing out a Spanish air on the violin, Berle arose at his table and began singing "Night and Day."

He kept it up just long enough to get a laugh, then sat down.

Berle undertook a serious drama, "I'll Hit the High Road," in 1943, and the critics hammered it hard. Wilella Waldorf, the late critic of the New York *Post*, concluded her review of it by asking, "Is this one of Milton Berle's gags?"

"What do you have to say to Miss Waldorf?" I asked Berle.

"All I have to say to Miss Waldorf," he retorted, "is that I'll never eat any more of her salads."

Then he added, "But one critic was very nice to my play."

"In what way?" I asked.

"He didn't see it!" snapped Berle.

All his life, Berle had been getting ready to be "Mr. Television."

You've heard it said that he was a bust on radio and in the movies.

But can you call a $500,000-a-year man a bust? Berle spent the spring and much of the summer of 1946 clowning at the barnlike Carnival night club over on Eighth Avenue near Madison Square Garden, receiving from proprietors Nicky Blair and Toots Shor the thumping sum of $10,000 per week.

That was prior to the Las Vegas boom. No night-club comedian had ever received such a salary. Nor had any café comic ever worked so hard, or so well.

Elliott Roosevelt, a pub crawler in those pre-TV days, told Berle one night:

"You make $10,000 a week, all right, but you work so long, it comes down to 40 cents an hour."

"Public Energy Number One," as he was called, was a pleasure to watch. He worked two shows a night—each one 105 minutes long—and appeared in every act on the bill. I can still see him jumping out to introduce a pretty and shapely singer, Marian Colby, who later was on his TV show, and eventually got a TV show of her own.

"Here's a girl," he would say, "who is very well reared. . . . Looks good in front, too. . . ."

In an outfit with the pants falling off, he would sing and dance madly, or play a harmonica that got jammed in his mouth, or trade quips with anybody and everybody in the audience.

Though I knew Milton's jokes by heart in those days, I could drop in almost every night and get a new laugh from something he would say to a visiting celebrity.

One night Frank Sinatra, broken up by Berle's gags, wished to congratulate him on his act, and thrust toward him a vase of red roses from his table.

"You're too cheap to bring me Pinch Bottle—you bring me Four Roses!" sneered Berle.

Judge Sam Leibowitz was in the audience and Berle, who liked to single out his customers and speak to them, said, "Judge, my brother's a very successful lawyer, too. . . . He has his own ambulance."

You could never tell when Berle was making up a joke or snatching one from his prodigious memory.

It's a legend that as a boy Milton set out to learn ten jokes a day—and that when he saw a cat or heard somebody mention a cat, he could instantly think of a hundred or so gag lines about a cat.

It was only a matter of picking the best one, or on occasion, fashioning a slightly new one from one already well-known.

I recall the night that Berle opened at the Carnival.

Looking down from the stage at the packed and overflowing house, Berle saw a waiter pushing through the mob, with two tables lifted up on his shoulders and, at times, above his head. The legs of the tables were pointing at the ceiling.

Whether Berle had the waiter planted there, I'll never know, but anyway, he shouted:

"My God—what's that—a moose?"

It got a good laugh, and Berle almost never failed after that to use it.

He was also using at that time some of the lines which you heard him employ later on TV.

"Good evening, ladies and gentlemen," he would begin, "on behalf of the management of the Carnival, and believe me, I'd like to be half of the management of the Carnival. . . .

"Mind you," he'd continue, "mind you (Adolph Mind You). I just arrived from Florida. I flew up. My arms are very tired. They surely do gamble down there. You know that white flag above the Hialeah race track? That's my shirt. I just had good news from my real-estate broker in Florida. They found land on my property. I had a wonderful compartment in the train on the way down, but the conductor kept locking me in at every station. . . . Say, mister," he'd address a bald man at the ringside, "your head is shining right in my eyes. For a minute I thought you were sitting upside down."

Now we'll skip to September, 1948, when I had a chance in my column to be rather prophetic. I reported that Berle, who then called himself "Ham, Sweet Ham," had been making $15,000 a week at the Latin Quarter, despite the hottest summer in years, and was "getting the chance that may (or may not) make him the world's most famous funnyman.

"He soon starts regularly on *both* television and radio, becoming the first big comedian to attempt this in major fashion," I reported, adding that on TV he would be permanent M.C., or as he interpreted it, "mental case," of the "Texaco Star Theater," "best TV offered thus far."

"We New Yorkers, natives or immigrants, feel it's about time Milton gets appreciated everywhere," I continued.

"He got going in radio last year but his sponsor canceled on him.

"Then Texaco leaped in and snagged him for $11,000 a week to do both its TV and radio shows. He points out that in TV you have no script to follow but must remember everything. Besides, you're watching camera angles. But at $11,000 a week for forty weeks, he'll get paid $440,000 for his headaches."

It was about this time that all the jokes about Milton's money commenced. Six or seven years later, when people began making gags about Jackie Gleason's $11,000,000 deal with Buick, to replace Berle, it's quite likely that Berle, with his colossal memory, recalled that he had been through all these jokes long before.

The trouble was, most of us didn't remember them.

As a kid, Berle had used these snicker jokes about other people. "Ted Lewis suffered a serious fall off his annuities," for example.

And the people who went on Berle's early TV shows complained sometimes that they always seemed to be off camera. Their relatives, waiting in the neighbors' living room, in front of a brand-new seven-inch set, would not see them except as they got jostled off to the side somewhere.

"The man who said, 'Nothing is impossible' never tried to get between Milton Berle and a television camera," said a joke in my column at the time.

Loving company, or loving listeners, Berle always traveled with his writers, and sometimes he had five or six or a dozen.

But, in his favor, he never denied it.

"I believe in keeping my wits about me," he said.

One night Jackie Eigen, first of the disc jockeys, now a big man in Chicago at the Chez Paree, told Berle, "I've got neuritis."

"That's what I need, too—some neuritis," cracked Berle.

46

Occasionally he was ill, or thought he was. The pace was swift and grueling.

Finishing one of his TV shows, Milton staggered out of Studio 6-B and groaned to his manager, Irving Gray, "Ohhhhh, I'm going to fall . . . to fall . . . right down."

"You can't . . . you can't!" cried Gray.

"Don't tell ME if I can fall down or not!" commanded Berle.

Since Berle was the first big man on TV, the first "Mr. Television," he was also the first who had to defend his title—and against the whole world.

He and Jack E. Leonard, the fat comic, had an ad lib tussle one day in 1950 at the Friars'.

"Be careful, or you won't be on my television show," kidded Berle.

"A couple more shows like the last one, and YOU won't be on your television show!" Leonard kidded back.

Year after year, CBS tried to beat Uncle Milton down. I don't suppose many people will remember that one year their choice was Frank Sinatra. That was '51. Berle had been the King now for two or three years, and already the wise men were saying, "This is the year that Milton gets knocked off. . . ."

Frankie was in there to "buck Berle"; this was admitted. Today Sinatra might do much better. But in '51 he was still known as a singer; nobody knew he was going to become a celebrated actor.

There was a plumpish young comic over on Du Mont whom Sinatra decided to use as a guest star: a boy with a nice little reputation. His name was Jackie Gleason. Frankie arranged to give this rotund youngster a Cadillac to appear on one of his shows, pitted against Berle.

I asked Gleason one night, during the rehearsals with Sinatra, "Do you ever run into Berle?"

"No," he said, "but I'd like to run over him . . . with my Cadillac."

Through all this, Berle was rather stoical.

"You have to expect competition," he said.

47

The Sinatra show never got off the ground. It was a mistake.

Berle kept plowing along, turning in huge ratings. His love for acting hadn't been in the least dimmed by all this wear and tear. He had a good friend, Irving Mansfield, creator of a show called "This Is Show Business," which had a long run. Mansfield's panel, you might recall, included George S. Kaufman, Clifton Fadiman, and other wits. Mansfield wished to get Berle, then the hottest thing in America, to make a guest appearance. The following dialogue took place:

Berle: "I'm allowed to make ten appearances at $15,000 a week. Can you pay me that?"

M: "No."

B: "Can you pay me $10,000?"

M: "No."

B: "$8,000?"

M: "No."

B: "$5,000?"

M: "No."

B: "$1,000?"

M: "No."

B: "$500?"

M: "No."

B: "$100?"

M: "No."

Berle: "Can you let me have two free tickets for my mother?"

Mansfield: "Yes."

Berle: "Okay! It's a deal!"

Quite aware of the campaign to unseat him, Berle was giving audiences everything he had. He employed all his talents and all his scores of disguises and costumes. Frequently he got into female attire. One night, comedian Jack Carter, appearing at the Copacabana, told the crowd, "Milton Berle was in here tonight but I didn't recognize him—he had men's clothes on."

Belittlers of his ability were numerous.

"What's Berle really got?" one of them asked his friend and writer at the time, Bobby Gordon.

"A lot of money!" replied Gordon.

Berle was the first big hirer of guest stars. He knew virtually everybody important, through his years of entertaining free at big charity benefits. One Sunday afternoon in February, 1951, he put in a phone call to Washington for then Vice-President Alben Barkley.

"Hello, V.P.," Berle greeted him.

"Hello, T.V.," answered Barkley. "What can I do for you?"

That simply, Berle got the Vice-President to participate in an Abraham Lincoln tribute on the show.

It was natural that there should be contract problems with such a big star. Texaco was extremely elated to be at the top of the TV heap . . . but one night Berle dropped a little story in my lap.

"I may not be back with Texaco in the fall," he said. "We've had a few misunderstandings."

They were straightened out . . . the sponsor paid Berle an increase and also gave him more authority over his own show . . . and NBC hastily thrust at him a new lifetime contract. During this period, around the Madison Avenue ad agencies or on Broadway, you heard the expression, "Berle owns Tuesday night." The NBC Tuesday eight-to-nine time belonged to him and NBC couldn't have switched him out of it if for some strange reason it should have wished to do so.

Each year his salary was going up. Escalator clauses in his contract and in the TV unions' contracts made the show more and more expensive as new stations opened.

By 1953, his salary boomed to $20,000 a week and then on to $25,000. Texaco said the tab was too high, so Buick jumped in and took over "lock, stock, and Berle." Berle was in the 91-per-cent income-tax bracket; he split up his pay somewhat, taking over some of the writing costs, some of the production costs, anything to help his show.

Nobody could say he didn't live good. He had a $150-a-week cigar bill. He got rid of about twenty to twenty-five cigars a day, and usually they cost a dollar each.

"The worst of it is," sighed his manager, Irving Gray, most sadly, "he only smokes them halfway down."

On December 9, 1953, Berle took time out to get married to Ruth Cosgrove, a former public-relations expert, who has helped greatly to steer his life since.

Undoubtedly the wedding reception at a hotel was the Broadway social event of the year.

It started in mid-forenoon, and some of the guests were still there with champagne glasses in their hand toward dusk. Berle himself wasn't in good shape due, as usual, to overwork.

Right at the reception's peak, the bridegroom announced: "I have to change my clothes."

"Why?" I asked. He was beautifully dressed, with a flower in the lapel.

"I'm soaking wet," Milton replied, grimly, and vanished for fifteen to twenty minutes.

As five hundred guests swirled through three big rooms, Henry Slate commented, "Berle just sent out for a hundred more extras."

A cake a couple of stories high was pushed forward.

"They're doing the cake bit," said one guest, adding, "Milton, you can't have your it and eat cake, too."

Along came comedian Gene Baylos toting a huge empty champagne bottle—a jeroboam.

"I'm going to take this back and get the deposit," he announced. "You lock up, Milton!

"Besides, I got to go to another wedding next door—Bishop Sheen married them."

That was a reference to the fact that Bishop Fulton J. Sheen was then on TV on Tuesday nights, opposing Berle. Milton had a lot of jokes about that situation. He wished, for example, that he could steal some of the bishop's four ace writers: Matthew, Mark, Luke, and John.

But Milton was doing very little kidding on this wedding day, for he was half sick, half full of penicillin.

Off to one side, he sang a song to his bride, one he'd composed, entitled "You'll Always Be Sure of Me." Milton's own comment was, "This is forever. It says so on the ring."

Everybody hoped so, figuring the comedian who'd made so

many millions laugh was entitled to some happiness of his own.

The Berles honeymooned in Miami. Ruth carried a special purse which I took careful notice of. It contained something not usually found in ladies' purses:

Cigars for her husband.

After a couple of years, and a lot of urging by NBC, Uncle Miltie is trying to take life easier. His lifetime contract was probably the first one ever given by any network, and he hasn't a thing to worry about. So does he rest? Oh, sure. . . . He decided to work night clubs a little in Miami Beach and Las Vegas!

DINAH SHORE'S

VITAL STATISTICS:

Born March 1, 1917, in Winchester, Tenn. Real name, Frances Rose Shore. Borrowed "Dinah" from song of same name as done by Ethel Waters, her favorite vocalist. Attended grade school in Nashville; graduated from Vanderbilt University. Married George Montgomery in Las Vegas, December 5, 1943. Has daughter, Melissa Ann (Missy), and son, John David (Jody).

Height, five feet four and a half inches; weight, 117 pounds; very auburn hair.

Doesn't smoke or drink. She's an excellent cook, as is George Montgomery. Her favorite dish, spaghetti.

Hobby, refinishing antique furniture, inherited from George.

They raise chickens, turkeys, ducks, on Encino ranch. She also loves going to movies and taking heavily scented baths.

Honors include Best Dressed Woman in Show Business, Emmy Award, Best Popular Female Vocalist, 1955 Woman of the Year.

RCA Victor recording star.

DINAH'S DYNAMITE

Perhaps you can imagine how flattered I was when Dinah Shore phoned *me* one morning about nine-o'clock at the Beverly Hilton in Beverly Hills.

I was already up, showered, shaved, and cologned for a ten-o'clock date with Dinah.

"This is Dinah," she announced, though it was really unnecessary to announce that famous voice. "Don't you eat any breakfast!"

I hadn't. She'd invited me to breakfast. But, just like her, she'd thought maybe I'd forgot the interview was to include breakfast. And she wanted to warn me to arrive hungry.

I knew from this call that I was going to set my diet back about a week—for we were going to have a sample of some Southern hospitality, and some Hollywood conversation.

And we did, although the conversation was difficult—not that Dinah ever lacks for words.

When we pulled in the driveway of the beautiful new home with the overhanging palms, I saw four cars already there.

"What's this . . . a party?" I wondered.

As I walked through the leaf, cool morning, I was startled by an enormous racket. It was at times so loud that it seemed to resemble a gangland murder massacre on television—and at other moments it suggested that maybe the Fourth World War had commenced right on Dinah's doorstep.

"That can't be Dinah rehearsing," I remarked to a friend who'd brought me.

"Maybe it's George firin' off some of his shootin' irons for a Western," allowed my companion.

Dinah opened the door herself, and her first words after the greeting were, "You'll have to pardon the noise."

"Is George all right?" my friend asked her.

"Sure, George is all right," Dinah retorted. "What made you ask that?"

"We sort of figured from the racket," my friend explained, "that maybe you were shootin' him."

Dinah laughed. "You see," she said, pointing, "we had to get rid of that tree."

Through a glass doorway looking out onto a swimming pool, I could see some workmen cutting down a tall palm with a power saw.

It was the power-sawing that caused the noise. The workmen would saw awhile, then rest, then resume, and when the

54

saw was sawing, it sounded like a riveter who might have planted his riveting machine two inches from your ear.

"George is replacing it with a Hawaiian palm like one we saw in Honolulu," Dinah told us. "If there's anything I hate to do, it's cut down a tree. But this one was going to ruin our pool."

Then I saw George out at the pool edge. He's still a boyish, good-looking, six foot three, and though he may give the impression of being less ebullient than Dinah from Dixie, he has a quiet sense of humor that is discerning and enjoyable.

George came indoors, shot out a big fist in a playful salutation, then disappeared, while I sat down to await the feast.

"You ready for breakfast?" Dinah asked me.

"I sure am!" I replied.

"George!" she called out through the house. He didn't answer, so we sat down anyway in a dining nook at a heaping table, on which I observed hot Southern biscuits, ham and eggs, sausage, plentiful supplies of rich-looking jams and jellies . . . and also some big French doughnuts. There was ample opportunity for a fellow who didn't care about his waistline to eat a 5,000-to-10,000-calorie breakfast there, and though I do care about my waistline, I ate it, anyway.

All the time the power saw was roaring away, slicing down the tree.

George finally sat down alongside me. "Isn't there anything we can do about the noise?" Dinah asked him appealingly from across the table.

"Sure, let the tree stay there," grinned George.

"WHAT'D YOU SAY?" Dinah yelled back at him. "I CAN'T HEAR A THING YOU'RE SAYING."

"I CAN'T HEAR A THING YOU'RE SAYING, EITHER!" George roared back.

"HAVE SOME MORE SAUSAGE!" Dinah yelled at me.

It was my turn to yell.

"IS THIS SOUTHERN SAUSAGE?" I boomed out.

"YES, IT IS," bellowed Dinah. "I BROUGHT IT ALL THE WAY FROM TENNESSEE."

"BUT I LIKE IT ANYWAY!" screamed George, who likes to heckle his wife about her Southern upbringin'.

"TRY ONE OF THOSE DOUGHNUTS!" Dinah ordered me.

"OH, I COULDN'T POSSIBLY EAT ONE," I answered.

So I ate two.

I got up groaning and suggested to Dinah that I'd better have some exercise.

"ALL RIGHT, WE'LL DO THE TOUR," she said.

At a fast, businesslike pace, she swept me through the beautiful house. As I went with Dinah from room to room, I felt it must be true, as people said, that this was the home of the happiest couple in Hollywood. George had gone off somewhere to handle some of his head-of-the-house duties. And now about every other sentence of Dinah's contained some extremely proud reference to her husband.

The tree-sawing had silenced for a while, and we could now talk normally.

"Look at this wonderful bed stand that George made for me," Dinah said when she came to their bedroom. "George laid out the pool himself," she said, when we came to that. . . . "He really built the whole house. Look at this painting George did. Isn't he talented? . . . Here's George's wardrobe. See how orderly everything is. . . . . Isn't he neat? I wish I were!"

In George's bathroom (I think it was), Dinah indicated, on the ceiling, a bar.

No, no, not a drinking bar.

A bar for exercising the muscles.

"That's where George chins himself," she explained.

"Do you ever chin yourself?" I asked Dinah.

"Sometimes, but I have to be careful about getting too muscular. I suppose you know that Mr. America is jealous of me now."

And she flexed her muscles to show how athletic she is.

"Now," she said, "we're going into my own rehearsal room and studio. . . ."

It wasn't large, but it was the expression of a good idea—a room for the "lady of the house." In one corner there was a record-player and television set . . . and in another there was an easel with an unfinished painting on it. Several "early Dinahs" hung on the wall.

"I turn on the record-player in here, and paint, and relax," Dinah said.

"I can also vocalize in here and not drive everybody crazy."

Her painting seemed excellent to my eye, although I know no more about art than a hog does about Sunday School. Dinah insisted that George's paintings are much better than hers, and as we walked out of the little studio, she stopped before one painting—a snow scene—and said, "George says that's the best one I've ever done . . . and it was my first one."

"Maybe he's biased because he comes from the snow country," I said.

"Now," remarked Dinah, "if you promise you won't faint, I'll really show you something. . . ."

I suddenly stood on the threshold of what seemed to be a woman's department of a department store. It could almost have been a dress shop.

"This is *my* wardrobe," Dinah told me . . . although I confess I had begun to suspect it was hers rather than George's inasmuch as there must have been 200 dresses hanging there.

Maybe there were 300, maybe 400.

All I know is that the rows seemed endless. They were outfits, or costumes, rather than just dresses, and some of them were several years old. I'd heard fascinating tales of actresses talking their studios out of special outfits the studios had bought for them, but I would like to be the last one to hint of such a shenanigan on the part of Miss Dinah Shore.

"There are my shoes," mentioned Dinah.

I swung around quickly, and saw a stack of footwear that must have been a quarter of a mile high.

"All my costumes aren't here," Dinah remarked, in an offhand way.

"You needn't apologize," I replied. "A couple hundred outfits don't assure a girl being actually well-groomed, I suppose, but it seems to me they would prevent you from going around in rags and tatters."

"It's not that," Dinah said. "My bigger costumes aren't

here . . . because you can't get them in the house. They're down at the studio."

"Doing what?"

"Just hanging there."

"Just *hanging* there?" I echoed.

"Sort of their *hangout*," replied Dinah. Pun my word, she did.

This is what TV has done for Dinah. Over the last couple of years, she has become an NBC fixture on TV, and her audiences love her for her wholesomeness. Dinah probably didn't know just how wholesome she was, until on one show, she sang "Lola," all about Lola getting what Lola wanted. A torrent of mail objected to Dinah being too sexy. For the simple reason that Dinah had a great drove of children watching, a fact she hadn't thoroughly appreciated.

"I didn't know about this big child audience I had," she told me.

"Well," observed the friend who'd come along with me, "I know that in our house, the kids have two favorites."

"Yes?" asked Dinah anxiously.

"Dinah," answered my friend, "and Pinky!"

Seeing Dinah in this colossal prosperity nudged me into going back into my memory and having a gander at the Southern belle a decade or more before.

'Twas 1942, and the slim-waisted, soft-voiced blues singer —as we called them then—was at the Paramount Theater in New York, reportedly being paid $1500 a week.

Three years before that, in 1939, she'd been willing to give it all up and go back to Nashville and become a social worker as her daddy had wished.

Daddy'd have been overjoyed if it had happened because, being a Southern gentleman, he was crestfallen about things appearing in the papers about Dinah.

For it looked to him—from the papers—as though Dinah had cornered most of the males in New York and was being wooed by scores and scores of them simultaneously.

Once he read that she had unquestionably fallen for So-and-so, and was crooning her love tunes to him.

He wrote her a rather severe letter in which he inquired whether she wasn't maybe going too far . . . and did she know the young man's family?

"Know his family!" retorted Dinah. "I don't even know him!"

Dinah had engaged a couple of press agents who didn't know a lot about Southern womanhood. Each and every night she was tripping gaily through the night clubs with this or that wolf—according to the gossip columns, which were fed by her press agents.

One day she read how she was sitting drearily, anxiously by her radio each Saturday afternoon, praying that her heart of hearts, Tim Lansing, the Fordham end, wouldn't be crippled for life playing football.

This was considered news by the columnist who ran it— in fact, it was considered news even by Dinah, since she hadn't met Tim yet.

When they did meet, eventually, Dinah thought to herself, "That's a familiar name"—not realizing that this was the man she was supposed to marry, according to the gossips. It was as phony as the rest. She said both hello and good-by to Tim the same night, their "romance" consisting of a fast nod.

Dinah was making a passel of money in those days for such a young gal.

She was getting $300 a week on the Eddie Cantor show, $500 a week on the Bristol-Myers program, and her records were already selling and paying her possibly $200 a week. Such jobs as the $1500-a-week chore at the Paramount lifted her into a very cozy income bracket.

Dinah'd also avoided the managerial traps that young ladies innocently fall into.

Rather, she'd escaped from one.

Before she really got started on Broadway, she felt she needed a manager . . . indeed, she thought having a manager would be just WONDERFUL . . . no matter how much a manager cost.

"So I got me TWO managers," she informed me. "And all I had to give them was 35 per cent of my earnings.

"Unfortunately, at the time, I didn't have any earnings."

Dinah discovered that the managers weren't doing anything for her. She therefore asked them in rather direct fashion just what their plans were for her.

"They said they were going to keep people away from me after I got a job," she said.

"I said I couldn't understand the need of that; so many people were keeping away from me already that I couldn't get a job.

"I talked them into freeing me from my contract.

"After all, I was getting nothing. As 35 per cent of nothing was nothing, what could they lose?"

Her career has in fact been "real crazy."

First, there was her name . . . Frances Rose Shore.

"Everybody down in Nashville was fond of calling me Fanny instead of Frances, and that was a very punny name," Dinah remembered.

"They'd say 'Fanny sat on a tack. Fanny Rose. Fanny Rose sat on a tack. Did Fanny rise? SHORE!' I just had to do something.

"So I changed my name to Dinah, because I'd sung 'Dinah' a lot when I went to Vanderbilt.

"I really stole my rendition of 'Dinah' in those days by listening to an Ethel Waters record. I guess I shouldn't use such impolite language, but the honest truth is, I swiped it."

Resisting her father's pleas that she go into social work, like any young lady should, she persuaded him to give her some money to try New York for a few weeks.

"I stayed at the Barbizon-Plaza and had my meals sent up. . . . Pretty soon I had only a couple of dollars left.

"I could no longer say, 'Charge it to Daddy.' Another girl and I got an apartment, and pretty soon we were living on bread and cheese—except when we got invited out to dinner.

"New Year's Eve came.

"The bread and cheese was all gone.

"I went up to a radio station—where I was singing for nothing—as was common in those days—and found out about a job that would pay $25 for one night's singing in Westchester.

"I actually had 10 cents left.

"Bus fares were a dime then, and the subway cost a nickel.

"Being extravagant, I rode the bus home. When I got to the apartment, I found a message saying the Westchester date was off.

"I was actually stony broke.

"I called Daddy and said I'd come home but meanwhile would he wire me $5 so I could eat. He wired me a lot more and told me if it meant that much to me, I could stay."

She kept on trying. Leo Reisman, Xavier Cugat, Tommy Dorsey, Ben Bernie, and other maestros liked her singing style.

Maybe you remember her low, slow singing of "Jim," "Yes, My Darling Daughter," "Blues in the Night," and "I Got It Bad and That Ain't Good." They became big records.

Dinah's often credited Vic Knight, former radio producer for Eddie Cantor, now a Los Angeles music publisher and head of a record company, with giving her one of her very biggest breaks.

He spotted her talent immediately.

Eddie Cantor was holding tryouts for girl singers.

"Vic arranged it so that I would be the only girl singer there for his tryouts. Mr. Cantor seemed to like my singing, and I went on his program."

Knight has denied there was anything unusual about that. "I knew Dinah was talented, and so why waste Eddie's time listening to girls who weren't?" he says.

Now that she earns as much as she does, and is almost as precious to NBC as the RCA Building, the magnolia-talkin' Dinah enjoys looking back to the days when she got $50 a week with Lennie Hayton's orchestra—and to certain of her pitfalls and pratfalls on the air.

Dinah, for example, was bounced off her first commercial radio program by one of the champion bouncers of all time.

The late George Washington Hill fired her three weeks after she'd been on "The Half and Half Tobacco Show." She got the ax because Mr. Hill, later immortalized in *The Huckster*, felt she wasn't belting a song as loud as it should be belted.

Broadway's poet laureate, Nick Kenny, had penned a song

entitled "Leanin' on the Old Top Rail," which Dinah sang neither loud enough nor fast enough in the opinion of music-lover Hill.

"I made up my mind I'd never sing on one of Mr. Hill's programs again," says Dinah.

"I daresay Mr. Hill made up his mind to the same thing."

Came a day when Dinah was beseeched to sing on "Your Hit Parade," also sponsored by Mr. Hill's tobacco enterprises.

What a chance! Did Dinah humbly agree to the offer?

She did—providing Mr. Hill would rip the rubber band off his roll and pay her $2500, whereas she normally got about $150 for such efforts.

"That'll show him how I feel about him tellin' me how to sing a song," thought Dinah.

And she naturally assumed she'd never hear about *that* again.

Instead, "Your Hit Parade" took her up on her price. She "like to fainted" but went on and sang, anyway—there was nothing else she could do—although it was an agonizing night because she kept thinking Mr. Hill would phone and fire her again even though she'd only been engaged for one evening.

Particularly annoying to Dinah was Mr. Hill's contention that she hadn't sung loud enough—because she'd been cheer leader down at Hume Fogg High in Nashville, and if it was yellin' he wanted, she could yell!

Dinah first fell for George Montgomery when she saw him on the screen.

She'd gone to Atlantic City to do nine shows a day in a Milton Berle show. Between shows, she dropped into a Boardwalk movie and saw the handsome George emoting.

"He's for me," Dinah said to herself, in effect.

It was in 1942—some years later—that she met him. She was at the Hollywood Canteen, singing for the GIs, when she saw him.

"He was with a blonde and I hated that girl on sight," Dinah says. There was nothing much she could do about it that night, but she saw him later, got introduced, and permitted him to discover that he had the same chemical reaction to her that she had to him.

On December 5, 1943, George dragged the magnolia miss to the altar in Las Vegas. He was in the Army then (he eventually was a sergeant), and they got wed while he was on leave from Alaska.

"Dinah looked mighty good after all those Eskimos," George says.

For five years, Dinah made personal appearances only on camp shows. She was the GIs' favorite gal singer; she'd drop in at a camp and say, "Well, boys, what do you want to hear?" —and the show would be on.

Just before the war ended, Dinah was used by the War Department as a psychological weapon.

The Army had her sing to the German soldiers—via radio— in French, German, and Danish.

She'd start with a little speech in which she said, "German soldiers! This is Dinah Shore. I have just returned from Paris, where I sang for the American troops. Meanwhile, our boys have entered Germany to reestablish order, freedom, and justice. I hope they will succeed, for then you will be able to return to your Fatherland and your families and start a new life."

She sang "I'll Get By," changing the lyric so that it said the Americans would get by the German lines. Her closing song was "I'll Be Seeing You."

Comedian Sammy Walsh accompanied her on the tour and complained that this kind of treatment was too good for the enemy.

"Maybe we're trying to kill them with kindness," he philosophized.

When Dinah was tapped for TV in 1951, she was ready— and she was an immediate hit.

"Dinah Shore has begun her own television program over NBC and it should be one of the delights of the season," correctly prophesied Jack Gould in the New York *Times* on December 3, 1951.

Gould spoke of her "greater maturity as an artist and performer," said she was "the picture of poise and naturalness," and added that she "wisely holds the chitchat down to a minimum and lets her songs speak for themselves."

"Back in the days of radio, she was often handicapped in reading lines and, indeed, the titans of Hollywood tended to write her off as primarily a record star," continued Gould.

"Hollywood," he concluded, "had better have a second look at Miss Shore."

But Dinah has been against letting them have a second look—George does the movies for the family. With Melissa (or Missy) and an adopted son, Jody, almost seven years younger, to occupy her in addition to TV and radio, Dinah has a crowded life.

It's so packed that in January, 1955, she rehearsed on a cross-country train for her personal appearance at the Waldorf-Astoria. A window had to be removed from the 20th Century Limited to take off a piano that she and her accompanist, Ticker Freeman, used en route.

The piano was squeezed into her apartment. She, Freeman, and the Skylarks rehearsed for many hours, though it wasn't easy for Ticker to play under such crowded conditions.

There wasn't room for a chair so he played on his knees.

Dinah traveled with considerable luggage, befitting a girl chosen by fashion designers as the "best-dressed woman in show business. . . ."

Dinah—who always answers the phone, "Mrs. Montgomery" now—has gone from a dime to millions of dollars. It's been quite a voyage.

Fanny Rose Shore Shore Has Rose.

There's one more point that I must not forget to bring out about the Rise of Rose.

Her quiet social life.

Dinah and George often allege that they're the dullest couple in Hollywood because they don't drink, smoke, or carouse around.

"I've never smoked, and I gag at the smell of liquor," says Dinah. "It's the same with George. When we go to a party, we try to figure out how soon we can get out, because we know we're so dull.

"At parties, when we ask for a soft drink, the host and hostess usually raise their eyebrows and keep them raised for the rest of the evening.

"Then they start talking to us about social conditions or politics in Pakistan or something. Because anybody who doesn't drink is supposed to be a horrible square—not supposed to be, but is.

"And the strange thing is that some people try to *make* us drink."

Dinah was expounding on this point one night to an acquaintance, who told her that she really should drink . . . it would relax her.

"Why is it that people try to make you drink when you don't want to?" she pleaded with this man. "Why is it if you don't like onions, nobody tries to force you to eat onions?"

"Onions," spoke up the drinking advocate, "are very good with martinis. How about an onion right now with a martini around it?"

"You see?" said Dinah. "George and I are hopeless!"

They may be, but they also seem to be completely happy, if that's possible in this life.

GROUCHO MARX'S

VITAL STATISTICS:

BORN—Wouldn't you like to know?

AT—Twilight.

TRUE NAME—Truman.

ALIAS—Harry Truman.

FATHER'S OCCUPATION—Bum.

FATHER'S PREOCCUPATION—Dames.

EDUCATION—I ain't had none.

RELIGION—Hindu.

HEIGHT—Well over five feet.

WEIGHT—Till the sun shines Nellie.

CHILDREN—Dionne Quintuplets and the Dolly Sisters.

OUTSTANDING ACHIEVEMENT—Ran the 100 yards the same day.

BOOKS YOU HAVE WRITTEN—*War and Peace* and *Winnie the Pooh*.

NAMES OF GHOST WRITER OF YOUR BOOKS—Shakespeare.

BOYHOOD AMBITION—To be a girl.

POLITICS—Populist.

CLUBS YOU'RE MOST FAMILIAR WITH—Policemen's.

FAVORITE COCKTAIL—Molotov.

"THE GREAT GROUCHO"

"These lifetime contracts they're giving television stars don't mean anything," Groucho Marx said to me not long ago at lunch.

"No?" I said, willingly playing his straight man.

"No . . . because no television star will ever live a lifetime."

Groucho was referring to the furious and at times almost killing pace that must be maintained by the stars who get ulcers and heart attacks fighting to keep their ratings up. Witty though the remark was, it didn't apply to Groucho, whose "You Bet Your Life" program constantly has a high rating—apparently with very little work being required from Groucho or anybody else. If you can believe him (and it's true, you can't all the time), he's the biggest loafer in Hollywood, television is a snap and a swindle, and they ought to arrest him for stealing the money from NBC and his sponsors.

"I laugh at how easy it is," Groucho said, "compared to what some of these other fellows go through.

"I suppose all the effort is necessary. Yet I sometimes wonder why it is—as Goodman Ace points out—that a show must always open with thirty-eight dancers, even though you can only see three dancers on your screen."

Presumably just about everybody knows that Groucho comes out without even three dancers. He just sits or stands there smoking a cigar, shoots his eyebrows up mischievously, leers occasionally, and bounces jokes off of quiz contestants, who seem to love him no matter how close he comes to insulting them.

Each year the experts hop onto their typewriters with both fingers and begin worrying about the "new comedians." It's usually May.

Each year about that time, Groucho's in New York, having filmed all his shows for the season and being occupied with nothing much but resting, seeing some shows and some baseball games.

And he notices how the experts are worrying about the "new comedians."

"Why doesn't somebody worry about us old comedians?" he lamented to me, kiddingly, one day. "Doesn't anybody care about what happens to us? I guess they've resigned themselves to seeing me doing my show someday from a wheelchair."

This gave him another idea, which he pounced on and developed.

"George Burns and Jack Benny and I will be like Civil War veterans," he suddenly decided. "Every year there'll be one less as we totter down Fifth Avenue."

The fact is, however, that Groucho's show is one of the few that is given a chance to last as long as its star lasts on earth. Groucho, therefore, could be a "lifetime star." When the geniuses in the ad agencies say, "I'd give that show two seasons," they never mean Groucho's show. They just assume, as Groucho puts it, that he'll be there forevermore.

And the reason for this, of course, is that Groucho has a built-in wit and doesn't need to be provided with a portable gag writer, or five or six of them. Sure, he uses some, but they'll all admit he's faster and funnier than they can ever be.

No matter how often you say this, people will continue to believe the opposite. So I will cite a couple of personal experiences.

On one of his spring visits to New York, I took Groucho to lunch at the Absinthe House, on West Forty-eighth Street, to sample some New Orleans cooking. We had just started out by taxi when Groucho got restless sitting there, in that stuffy cab, on a sunny day.

"Let's walk!" he suddenly said, hopping out.

Possibly he felt guilty leaving the cab without a fare—though the cabbie was well tipped—for he turned to three young girls and began giving them a selling talk as to why they ought to take this taxi to wherever they were going.

"It's a very nice cab," he orated. "I can personally recommend it. The driver is a fine fellow by the name of Frank Folsom."

(Folsom is chairman of the RCA Executive Committee.)

As we walked along, I mentioned that "our" movie, "Copacabana," in which I'd appeared for a minute or less, was appearing on TV all week. It was a picture Groucho remembered all too well.

"Yes, I've got a lot of fan mail about it—all threatening," he said.

When we arrived at the restaurant, I introduced Groucho to Mrs. Mark Rubin, co-owner of the restaurant, a charming and attractive young woman. Groucho at this point was unmarried and one of his first sentences to her went like this:

"Speaking of cooking, you're quite a dish."

"It's a great honor to have you with us," she replied bashfully.

"If it's such a great honor, cut out the balderdash and pick up the check!" exclaimed Groucho.

The waiter came over and was ready to take our order.

"How is that corned-beef hash?" Groucho asked.

"You can't go wrong," the waiter answered.

"Who's trying to go wrong?" thundered Groucho. "It's too early in the day for that. I merely asked you, is the corned-beef hash any good?"

Groucho watched Mrs. Rubin being admired by a man from Nebraska, who picked up her hand and held it as he was lingering over his leave-taking.

"Is that part of the lunch—lady's-fingers for dessert?" asked Groucho.

"Well, how was the food?" Mrs. Rubin asked as we got ready to go.

"I'll let you know in a couple of hours," Groucho said.

Groucho then said to Mrs. Rubin, "There's only one thing I want to say to you."

"What's that?"

"I'm sorry you're married!"

On another unforgettable occasion, we had lunch at Romanoff's in Hollywood, and Groucho began by ordering sherry.

"That's all I'll have," he said, "because you can't be on television and drink."

Thinking it over, he added, "And you can't be on television and not drink!"

The conversation continued along those lines, for Groucho as usual had arrived with a lot of quips on his shoulder.

"Would you care to see a menu?" the waiter asked.

"No, I've eaten here and I don't care if I never see another one of your menus," snapped Groucho.

"Bring me some liver, but be careful whose it is, because I know a lot of people who've left their livers in here at the bar," Groucho told the waiter. "I want it so well-done, and burned and charred, that I won't know it's liver I'm eating unless somebody tells me, and I'll thank you to keep your mouth shut."

My wife was studying the menu.

"I think I'll have the ham," she said.

"ARE YOU REFERRING TO ME?" demanded Groucho.

On still another luncheon date, a waiter said to Groucho, "The rolled pancake is very nice."

"Listen," growled Groucho, "if I ever roll anything, it won't be a pancake."

It was on this occasion that Groucho told me he was going to have an elaborate dinner for me at his home. He would have many movie celebrities there and some delicious cocktails and much wondrous food. How would next Thursday be? About eight o'clock?

"Fine," I said, enthusiastically.

"Then, it's all set. Be there not later than eight."

"Right," I said. "By the way, what's the address?"

"Wouldn't you like to know?" shot back Groucho.

Of course he did give us the address, and the dinner was a big success—at least from my standpoint, for I got a look at Groucho in his own home and saw him as a very serious man at times. He spoke at length of Will Rogers, whom he'd known well, and discussed politics, in which he's extremely interested. Groucho felt that Rogers, when he got famous, had to be traveling so much that he sacrificed all home life, all ties with his family. This Groucho never wanted to do.

There was a zany kind of relationship within the family, which Groucho's son, Arthur, later described in a book.

For example, when the family went abroad, Groucho recited history at each historic landmark. At the Tower of

London, Groucho said, "Now, this is where Henry the Eighth had all his wives' heads chopped off. It was cheaper than paying them alimony."

Groucho went to the Stock Exchange once and, at the height of the trading, arose, cleared his throat, shot up his eyebrows, and began singing, "When Irish Eyes Are Smiling."

An attendant sought to restrain him.

"Listen, you crooks," shouted Groucho, "you wiped me out of $250,000 in 1929. For that kind of dough, I'm entitled to sing if I want to."

This wonderful impudence is pure Groucho and Groucho at his best. When he and his brothers were together in "Cocoanuts" in Washington many years ago, Groucho leaned out over the footlights one night and addressed President Coolidge, who was in the audience.

"Aren't you up past your bedtime, Calvin?" Groucho asked.

Groucho ad libbed so much in that show that playwright George S. Kaufman, the author, commented once toward the end of the long run, "I may be wrong, but I think I just heard one of the original lines!"

Groucho's great success on TV has finally given him a feeling of security—strangely, during all those years when he already was so famous and so widely quoted, he kept fearing that he would wind up in the poorhouse or just as a broken down, broken up, and "broke" ham.

This demonstrates that he is really quite a serious man.

"I only had to look around me to feel that way," Groucho explained to me once. "In 1939, when we made 'A Day at the Races,' I remember there were twelve women working as extras who had once earned $1,000 a week or more.

"The thing scared me. I was terrified of having to work as an extra some day.

"So I took $25,000, all the money I had at the time, and put it into an annuity, which would pay me $80 a week when I reached fifty-five.

"That, I figured, would at least keep me off relief—although it wouldn't necessarily keep me from working as an extra!"

Many experts seemed to think Groucho was washed up—

as far as the air was concerned—when he launched his present show. He seemed to think, personally, that he wasn't meant for either radio or TV. Once when asked whether he preferred movies, the stage, or radio, he replied:

"Radio I like best. In the first place, nobody ever hears you."

Evidently he had to be seen to be appreciated. His TV chores—when he films his program before a studio audience— are about as screwballish as may be expected. For example, he may say to some visiting newspaperman, "They tell me you're one of the biggest columnists in the South."

"Thanks," the columnist may reply, feeling quite flattered.

"How tall are you?" Groucho'll exclaim next.

Maybe there's a fish peddler among the would-be contestants (as there was on one of my visits). He said he'd come in from the Fulton Fish Market, in New York City.

"How long did you flounder around there?" asked Groucho.

Next came a chiropodist.

"By the way," Groucho told him, "my wife's foot hurt this morning."

"Where did it hurt?" asked the chiropodist, helpfully.

"In the seat of my pants," retorted Groucho.

He asked an accountant, "How much is one and one?"

"Two."

"Wrong! Fourteen! I was thinking of one and one rabbit!"

Groucho once told me of his vast admiration for Gilbert and Sullivan and tipped off that his humor is something like that found in their works. He reminded me of an anecdote about Gilbert; how he once asked an associate, "Have you seen my wife?"

"I think she's around behind," the associate said.

"I'm aware of that!" barked Gilbert. "Have you seen her?"

Sometimes Groucho is better Gilbert and Sullivan than they were, in my opinion. I think of the time—again when he was single—when he was playing tennis with a pretty young girl. His style of play and his general good conduct pleased her.

"You're a man after my own heart," she told him.

"And that's not all I'm after," he told her.

His brother Chico declared one day, "The trouble with us Marxes is, we're oversexed."

"*You're* oversexed," cracked Groucho. "I'm over sixty."

These flashes of nonsense—and, occasionally, of good sense —come from God knows where. Back in his movie days, during a love scene, Groucho paused to ask the object of his desire what champagne she'd like to drink.

"Mumm's 28," the actress replied.

"I don't care how old your mother is!" snarled Groucho. "What kind of champagne do you want?"

The amazing thing about this amazing man is that there has been a Groucho Marx cult for more than a quarter of a century. Around 1930, there were people who would say, "Did you hear the last Groucho Marx crack?" And then they would repeat a line from a Marx Brothers movie or stage show, such as—there I go doing it!—"Waiter, have you any milk-fed chicken? Well, then milk one and bring it in!"

Or: "I shot a bear in my pajamas. How he ever got in my pajamas I don't know."

It may seem surprising that Groucho was a campaigner for the late Heywood Broun when Broun ran for Congress in New York. Well, maybe not a campaigner . . . but at least he wrote a speech for him . . . well, maybe not a speech exactly . . .

Groucho prepared an introduction for Broun, which he delivered at one of the Broun rallies.

The speech was such that it trickled all the way out to the Middle West, where I was a college student, and I got hold of a copy. There's no use to go into the entire speech, but some of it remains vastly amusing today.

"Man and boy, I have known Heywood Broun for thirty years," he began.

"He has known me for thirty years.

"This makes a total of sixty years and brings us down to the fiscal year of 1861, when conditions were much the same as they are now.

"My father was out of a job at the time, the farmers were complaining about the prices, and the Prices, who lived right next door, were complaining about my father. . . .

"And so, pupils of the Pratt Street Grammar School, we have come together today to observe Ann Arbor Day and plant a tree in honor of that great Polish explorer, Heywood Broun.

"Let us hope that one day the frozen Yukon wastes will give him up. Let us hope that something at least will give him up. Perhaps he will give himself up.

"I gave him up long ago. . . ."

(Incidentally, Broun wasn't elected.)

Many years later when Harry Truman was President, with very little likelihood that he would be dislodged, Groucho made a sharp political observation.

"It looks like the only way a Republican can get into the White House," he said, "will be to marry Margaret."

Of course Dwight D. Eisenhower came along then and that joke had to be retired. It was around that time that Groucho was widely quoted because he had turned down membership in the Friars Club in the most memorable letter the club ever received.

"I do not wish to belong to a club," he said, "which would have me as a member."

How could it have been said better? This again is pure Groucho. They tell another story of Groucho going once to a hotel which, he discovered on his arrival, was anti-Semitic. It wanted no Jews among its guests. So he signed the register, "Groucho McMarx."

"What an active life we led," he exclaimed once, telling about a hunting trip. "Up at six, breakfast at six thirty, back in bed by seven."

Watching his TV show, I often am struck by the affection that the contestants have for him. They have to have, or they would be angry. I remember once he was interviewing a girl from Australia.

"How did you get to the United States?" he asked her.

"I flew over by plane," she answered.

"That's a good way to fly," Groucho said. "A girl's a fool to fly any other way."

A young man was about to tell Groucho just how he and his wife had met.

"You see," the young man said, launching the tale, "I drive a truck."

"And you ran over her?" asked Groucho.

"No, no," interrupted the young fellow anxiously. "You see, she works in a restaurant."

"You drove the truck into the restaurant?" asked Groucho.

"Of course not! I drove the truck to a farm to pick up some turkeys. The farmer told me I'd find some turkeys out in the barn."

"And your wife was among them?" asked Groucho.

Unfortunately, all the dialogue that Groucho gets involved in with his contestants isn't permitted on the air. He is very expert at these slightly naughty lines. One night Groucho overheard a couple of women at his table engaging in a long, boring conversation about cooking.

"I made a stew last night for my dinner," one woman said.

"Anybody we know?" asked Groucho.

Groucho gave a party for S. J. Perelman and Al Hirschfeld once in Hollywood and insisted that the party be stag. Some of the guests invited didn't quite know how they could get away from their wives, but Perelman said, "I'll have no trouble, because my wife isn't in town, anyway."

"Get somebody else's wife so you can leave her at home!" ordered Groucho.

The Hollywood restaurateur Dave Chasen served strawberry shortcake. "It's a small cake," mentioned *Variety* editor Abel Green.

"It's a short cake but a merry one," amended Groucho. In a talk about Perelman which was supposed to be a testimonial-type speech, he said, "He's as comfortable to be with as an old glove, and just as interesting."

Personally, Groucho is a bundle of idiosyncrasies. Economy has always been his one big aim, since the stock-market crash. His son, Arthur, has told how Groucho undertook to save by using napkin rings at the table as his grandfather had done.

"If each person used a napkin the whole week, the laundry bills would be smaller," Arthur explained. "Father bought four of the most expensive sterling-silver napkin rings you could buy, and had our names engraved on them. This came to $113, but in the long run Father figured it would be worth it.

"In twenty years he probably would have saved at least $7 by using napkin rings."

The idea collapsed, anyway, about the third night, when Groucho screamed at the table, "Can't a person get a clean napkin around here?" Then he demanded that they get rid of the napkin rings at once, claiming they were old-fashioned and that he didn't like them. "Whose idea were they, anyway?" he wanted to know.

Groucho has some very mellow moments, however. If he goes to a Broadway show and sees a performer he likes, he may return to his hotel and write the performer a fan letter. Naturally, these are greatly treasured by actors.

One of Groucho's worries for some years was his big, black, painted-on mustache that he wore on stage and on the screen.

It, and the cigar, were sure to get him recognized almost anywhere in the so-called civilized world. But when he got tired of doing movies, I think he felt that the comedy mustache was a little beneath him. Perhaps, being a man of taste, he considered it a crutch, or a little corny.

Once when we had a date, during the early period of his casting off of the fake mustache, he said to me over the phone:

"You'll be able to recognize me. I'll be wearing a red dress."

Of course he has a real mustache, a small one, which he claims belongs to his maid. Before TV, Groucho's real face wasn't known. He would be able to go almost anywhere in New York—except maybe in Sardi's or Toots Shor's or Lindy's —and not be pointed out as Groucho Marx.

He did one or two movies without the prop mustache— then came TV—and I recall him telling me once, "Hey, I was in the Stage Delicatessen—and somebody recognized me."

I felt that it had given him a considerable little bit of

pleasure to be recognized by his own face finally . . . in his middle fifties.

Groucho doesn't get chummy with a lot of people. Ed Sullivan has been a friend, though, for a long time, and Ed likes to tell how he and Groucho once went for an auto trip.

That was also the day Groucho gave up golf.

After knocking five new balls into the Pacific while on the sixteenth hole at Cyprus Point course in Del Monte, Calif., Groucho took the remaining balls from the bag, threw them into the ocean, and then did the same with his golf bag and golf clubs.

Then the same day they started to drive from Beverly Hills to Pebble Beach—Groucho driving and following the playwright Norman Krasna, who is a rather fast driver.

"Every citizen should abide by the rules," Groucho said, holding his car down to about thirty miles an hour. "If he is lucky enough to be well known, his responsibility is even greater."

Sullivan heckled him from the back seat about his slow driving, and Groucho finally stepped on the gas on a hill trying to pass a truck.

A motorcycle cop shot up just then and angrily waved Groucho back into line.

"That's what happens," growled Groucho, "when you take advice from an idiot."

And he slowed down to twenty miles an hour . . . especially when Sullivan said there was a motorcycle cop on their heels.

It turned out that the man on the motorcycle was a Western Union messenger. Groucho then turned his wit on Sullivan, and Ed said, "Now even if I saw a motorcycle cop, I wouldn't tell you."

And just then he saw one, and didn't tell him. And for some reason—maybe because he was having too much fun returning Sullivan's needling—Groucho stepped on the gas . . . and the cop pulled up and motioned him over to the side of the highway.

The cop heard some uproarious laughter and demanded, "What's so funny about breaking the law?"

"That's not me laughing," said Groucho. "Those noises are from the back seat. I'm taking my half-wit brother-in-law to an insane asylum."

The cop looked into the back seat at the convulsed Sullivan.

"Has he been nuts long?" inquired the cop.

"Since birth," snapped Groucho.

But all this didn't stop Groucho from getting the first ticket he'd got in his life. He's still Sullivan's friend, though, proving that it takes a good bit more than a ticket for speeding to part Groucho from a pal.

Groucho told some of us once that the caution in his make-up came from his father . . . and, of course, he had a story to illustrate.

He maintained that his father, Sam Marx, an Alsatian who'd come to this country at seventeen and was the first tailor who ever managed without a tape measure, was in a theater lobby one day when he heard a man saying the Marx Brothers weren't really brothers.

Now Sam Marx, being the father, was a fairly good authority on the subject at issue, but he didn't end the argument . . . he just crept into it.

"I don't know anything about it, but I think they *are* brothers," said Sam Marx.

"And I say they're not," shot back the stranger in the lobby. "Two of them are brothers and two of them are cousins."

"I don't think so," said Sam Marx. "I think they're brothers."

"I'll bet you $10 that two are brothers and two are cousins!" exclaimed the stranger heatedly.

"What odds'll you give me?" asked Sam Marx.

Groucho has said that when he was born, an uncle of his named Julius "dropped everything, including two aces he had up his sleeve," and rushed over to the Marx flat. Thinking that Uncle Julius had money, Groucho's parents named their son Julius. Uncle Julius moved in with them and stayed around until Groucho was old enough to get married, always living in the best room in the house. He also owed Groucho's father $84, but when he died, he left them his entire estate, according to Groucho, consisting of nothing.

It was after they'd left grammar school and started out in vaudeville that a monologist named Art Fisher named the Marx Brothers Groucho, Harpo, and Chico. The apparent reason for calling Groucho by such a name is that even as a young man he could give the appearance of being stern or grouchy.

The oldest Marx Brother, Leonard, was named Chico because he was crazy about girls, who were then called "chickens." The next brother, Arthur, was called Harpo because he played the harp.

Groucho had a date with Gracie Allen—who wasn't yet married to George Burns—the night he met his first wife-to-be.

Ruth Johnson was then in her late teens and had applied for a job with the brother act.

A girl who'd been dancing with brother Zeppo had quit, and Zeppo had hired this attractive brunette as a replacement. Zeppo took her to dinner down at Luchow's on Fourteenth Street, famous then as now as a rendezvous for show-business names, and happened to find Groucho there with Gracie Allen.

"This is our new dancer," Zeppo said, introducing the girl to Gracie and Groucho.

"I want to congratulate you on your good taste," Groucho said to Zeppo as he looked the young girl up and down.

"And I wish, young lady, I could say the same to you," Groucho added. They were married soon after that and were an ostensibly happy married couple for around a quarter of a century. When they finally parted, with Mrs. Marx driving away, leaving Groucho standing there at the driveway alongside their house, Groucho said, "Well, it was nice knowing you, and if you're ever in the neighborhood again, drop in."

The first Mrs. Groucho laughed, and so the marriage ended on a smile. In 1945, Groucho married Kay Gorcey, the former actress, and they were divorced in 1950. Early in 1954, we began hearing rumors that Groucho was serious about a pretty brunette named Eden Hartford, but we didn't know how serious.

Miss Hartford had a sister Dee working in a picture, "A Girl in Every Port," with Groucho, when she dropped by the set in 1952 and met Groucho for the first time.

Not one to rush into things at this stage of his life, Groucho paid her such attentions as bringing her a glass of water but told her, "I'll call you in six weeks. I never go out when I'm working."

He did, too; he took her out for his favorite dinner, bacon, eggs, pumpernickel bread, and beer . . . and, well, they were married a couple of years later in Sun Valley, and honeymooned in Las Vegas.

"I played the slot machines a bit, but since the stockmarket crash, Groucho doesn't gamble," Eden Hartford Marx said in a magazine article.

"That's ridiculous," retorted Groucho. "I got married, didn't I?"

Now that people get excited about the Emmy award—TV's Oscar—it's interesting to note that Groucho won that in 1951.

Just before that, his radio show had won the Peabody Award, the radio equivalent of the Pulitzer Prize.

So it looks like everybody loves Groucho and nobody hates him. Though I suppose even this could be debated. Asked once whether any of his contestants have ever been mad at him, Groucho replied:

"No, they just go away happy, rich, and dazed. I just go away dazed. But that's the way I arrive in the first place."

The contestants do have a merry time. One, a chemistry teacher from California, was so good that Groucho told him:

"Doc, if you were smart, you'd quit your classroom and go into vaudeville."

"Well, Groucho," answered the teacher, "I'll confess that right now I've got my eye on your job."

"Yeah," flipped Groucho, "you may have your eye on it—but look what I've got on it!"

I guess Groucho's about the most independent TV star living—his independence extends even to his bosses. He's one of the people who can afford to turn down $100,000 to do a spectacular or to work in Las Vegas. He doesn't mind admitting publicly that he doesn't see much of his fan mail. If he finds some so-called important person a bore, Groucho's likely to tell him so, even though he may be influential. The rich make no impression on Groucho; after all, right now he's well-heeled himself.

Such is his stature that people enjoy being clobbered by his witty remarks and tell them afterward with great pride.

I know this to be true, for it has happened to me. I shan't forget—nor quit telling—of the experience in the movie "Copacabana" with him, when he looked in on Louis Sobol, Abel Green, and me, as we were undertaking our emoting.

"This is just a rehearsal," I apologized to him.

"That's all this picture will ever be—a rehearsal!" he said, stamping off.

Once he reviewed a book I had spent a couple of years writing and I was overjoyed to have him say, "I was very much surprised by one thing about the book—it was well written. I don't want to go overboard about the book, although I wish Wilson had before he wrote it."

Even his brothers, who must be a little angry at him by this time, finding him quoted always when they're not, secretly enjoy his barbs. And you'll find brother Chico quoting Groucho as telling about Chico's gambling.

"Chico got smart," Groucho said. "It only took him fifty years to find out you can't win. Some people are very bright and find out in only thirty-five years."

Perhaps even Clara Bow is happy about his comments about a fan letter he got from her.

"I couldn't help thinking," he said, " 'Why couldn't she have written to me thirty years ago?' You don't notice Anne Baxter writing to me. Why doesn't she? Doesn't she smoke the kind of cigars I smoke?"

Of all Groucho's witty but preposterous remarks that I've absorbed in my years of idol worshiping, the one that stands out again and again is alleged to have occurred when he and some friends went to see a movie that they were afraid was going to be very good.

They were fearful of its being excellent because it was, in a way, a competitor of the Marx Brothers' pictures.

They settled down in their seats to watch, and as soon as the title had flashed on, even before the opening scene, Groucho turned to his brothers and said, wearily:

"Drags, doesn't it?"

That life never does around Groucho.

ARLENE FRANCIS'

VITAL STATISTICS:

Born Arlene Francis Kazanjian on October 20, 1908, an only child, in Boston. Parents, Aram and Lea Kazanjian (father was a famous portrait photographer). Educated at Convent of Mount St. Vincent, Riverdale, N. Y.; Finch's Finishing School for Young Ladies, New York City; and America Theatre Guild School. Married Neil Agnew, film executive, in 1935, divorced in 1945; married Martin Gabel, actor-producer-director, on May 14, 1946. Religion: Greek Orthodox. Height, five feet six; weight, 123 pounds. Home address, Park Avenue, and Mt. Kisco, N. Y. Hobbies, reading, theater, likes being a housewife. Helped found and works for United Cerebral Palsy Association. Children: Peter (son with Martin Gabel).

ARLENE THE ARMENIAN

Arlene Francis was talking about Texas on one of her two television shows recently, and said, "The Texans are so cordial. You put your hand up to wave hello to somebody—and they put a drink in it."

Miss Francis has dropped literally thousands of such quips on the air she lives on in the last doze nyears, establishing herself as one of America's quickest wits—yet, strangely, women still like her . . . and so do men.

Wit is a dangerous possession, especially to women, for it scares men and makes other women jealous. But Arlene Francis has blended with it a talent for making people like her, and the result is unbeatable. The star of NBC's "Arlene Francis Show" is beloved not only by millions of male and female fans but also by the Department of Internal Revenue, to whom she reports around a quarter of a million dollars a year in earnings. Typically, Arlene will deny to you that she is a wit, alleging that she prattles so perpetually that naturally something amusing slips out occasionally.

"And as for me being on two networks—I guess anybody could be if they had as little sense as I have," she says. "I just happen to love work. I dig that the most."

A 6:45 A.M. riser who's often in bed at 9 P.M., this Boston-born daughter of a famous Armenian socialite photographer manages to get her fun from batting the verbal ball around on TV. She has the knack of getting to the point of a situation with an especially penetrating remark that turns out to be humorous.

One night when Miss Joan Diener, of the show "Kismet," one of the most opulent-bosomed young ladies ever to come out of Cleveland, was on a TV show, with a problem, Miss Francis took one pop-eyed look at her bodice, then tossed her head and remarked:

"My point of view is that you have not one but two problems."

Miss Francis was at a Washington Congressional dinner, with Vice-President Nixon present, when AP Correspondent Jack Bell, a great reporter, accidentally happened to introduce her as "Arlene Thomas."

Looking squarely at Mr. Bell, Arlene flipped, "Thank you, Mr. Ding Dong."

Arlene would have you believe that this quick quipping is hereditary; that her grandfather, Albert Davis, "a bit of a rake," died in Brookline, Mass., after coming out of a coma long enough to say to his wife from his deathbed, "I hear the rustle of a woman's skirt and I like to think that's the last thing I'll hear as I go out."

Few remember that Arlene was mistress of ceremonies of a radio show called "What's My Name?" and of another called "Blind Date" and that she even toiled in the violinyards as an M.C. for Phil Spitalny. When laughing about her age, which she doesn't go around mentioning, she says, "My uncle, Dr. Varazstad Kazanjian, of Boston, is the greatest plastic surgeon in the world. No other niece can make that statement. Please mention him because I may need him one of these days. He's seventy and I keep saying to him, 'Please, uncle, take good care of yourself.'"

Arlene's name is also Kazanjian, and her father, Aram, the photographer, who didn't want her to go into acting, lives now not far from the Park Avenue residence that Arlene and her husband, Martin Gabel, moved into not long ago.

Personally she toted beer and sandwiches to the workmen heeding her commands when she took over at decorating it, and overjoyed at her friendliness, they gladly worked overtime. It contains some treasured art pieces; most of them were not, however, painted by Arlene, who tried painting briefly at her father's insistence. She longed for greasepaint and when she played a male role in a girls' school play—hauling a girl thirty pounds heavier than she was around in her arms just to prove she could do it—the sisters of the Convent of Mount St. Vincent in Riverdale advised her father that he'd better not resist her stage aspirations any longer.

Considering the many quips she tosses off instantly, Arlene

gets into remarkably little trouble. "Her wit is not the wounding type," her husband says. One night, "What's My Line?" had Senator McClelland, of Arkansas, as a mystery guest. The panelists had discovered that the guest was a Democrat. "So you're not Senator McCarthy?" said Fred Allen. "No," replied McClelland.

"Congratulations!" commented Arlene, who of course meant it just the way it sounded.

So many protests came in from viewers that John Daly, moderator of the program, finally sent out a form letter saying Arlene merely had been congratulating Fred Allen for discovering that the mystery guest was not McCarthy.

Normally, though, the target of Arlene's wit is considerably warmed by it. When she and Gabel vacationed in France, they felt quite linguistic after having a French tutor come to their house for several weeks.

Visiting one restaurant, Gabel wanted merely a roast-beef sandwich.

He rattled off the order in such French that Arlene exclaimed in admiration, "Listen to him. He is ordering a roast-beef sandwich, and he sounds as though he were addressing the Chamber of Deputies calling for the dissolution of the government and you have the impulse to shout 'Bravo!'"

On an early "Home" show, Arlene went down with a cameraman in a cozy diving bell off Catalina Island.

Something went wrong with the pressure on the return to the surface, and the thing zoomed back up.

Dizzy but unshaken, Arlene managed to quip, "Now I know what it's like to be a champagne cork."

A diamond pendant that Gabel gave her and which she wears even while bathing has become almost as familiar a part of Arlene as her ad libs.

"Did you ever take it off?" I asked her.

"Only once."

"What happened?"

"It almost started a *scandale*."

"Tell me about it."

"I showed up on the program without it and got all those letters asking whether Martin had left me or what."

"Why didn't you wear it that time?"

"Chain broke," smiled Arlene.

Mrs. James Kilgallen, mother of Dorothy Kilgallen, heard it said "positively" in a beauty parlor one day that the pendant was always there on her neck because Arlene was deaf and it was really not a pendant but a hearing aid.

"Some day," said Arlene mischievously, "I'm going to hold it up to my ear and say, 'How was that, John?'"

To her husband, Arlene is almost as wondrous a personality as she is to the millions for whom she scintillates on TV. But, like many husbands, he has figured his wife out and analyzed her success—in this case, ungrudgingly and with genuine male admiration.

"How does she do all she does?" he often says, echoing a question. "Well, first of all, don't forget, she's the star.

"It's a case of walking into a red-carpet situation. She's a success and in a modest way she's aware that she's a success.

"In the morning, for example, there's a Cadillac and a liveried chauffeur from the Carnegie Hall Limousine Service waiting at seven forty-five to take her to the studio.

"Her secretary, Muriel Fleet, is constantly with her at the studio and at home or in the limousine. Beauty treatments are brought to her, designers frequently come to our home. In order that she may get so much done, it is necessary to bring many things to her."

Arlene finds herself in a "forced kind of luxury living," as Gabel sees it. She has time now for very few flings at cookery in her own kitchen. A married couple lives in, doing the housework, and a laundress comes in. The French tutor comes in and the dressmakers come in. About everything comes in except the program, and Arlene has such an attractive home that maybe that can be arranged.

A non-worrier, she figures that worrying, the ulcer-giving kind, wastes nervous energy that can be better applied to carrying out her heavy duties, including homemaking.

A friend dropped in on Arlene once at 9 P.M. and found her bent over her Bendix.

"It's got to be done," she explained.

On a vacation in Europe, work wasn't forgotten. She and Gabel went to the Cannes Film Festival and then to Rome to talk to Gina Lollobrigida about appearing in "Serenade."

"Lollo's so beautiful and so round—and her personality's so round, too," was Arlene's appraisal of the Marilyn Monroe of Italy.

She was impressed by Gina's willingness to take fencing lessons and vowed that she'd like to try it.

Gambling on that trip, they won "700 and something dollars" in francs and wanted to change it into lira, as they were heading for Italy.

"The prefect of police spoke no English—nuttin'—and Martin was there with his French dictionary—how much of a fight can you put up in a foreign language?" asked Arlene.

She gave her impressions of the dialogue.

"*Donnez-moi l'argent!*" . . . "*Mais le Douane Central ferme* for two hours." . . . "*Ferme!* You weren't *ferme* when you gave me the money two hours ago." . . . "*Je ne connais pas* what to do." . . . "You can say that again." . . . "Ah, *ici l'officer.*" . . . "Great. *Ouvrez la fenêtre* and *donnez-moi l'argent.*" . . . "*Oui, monsieur. Ici est votre* money." . . . "*Merci beaucoup,* fellow. You're nice people to deal with, and if I ever get in a jam like this again, it'll be my own fault." . . . "*Oui, monsieur. Merci beaucoup pour votre* kind words."

"And so," says Arlene, "we pocketed our loot and were soon on the *chemin de fer.*"

Arlene handles the family money. "So many do nowadays," she says. "I think women are all basically Hetty Greens at heart."

One week night on which Arlene permits herself the luxury of staying up as late as eleven is that on which there's a worth-while Broadway theater opening.

As theater critic for her TV program, Arlene does a 500-word review of the more important productions.

"Being an actress herself, she's pretty charitable," Gabel says. "But she would be, anyway, because basically she's a very decent girl. Television is a very intimate medium, and you can't fake charm—you eventually stand revealed."

The harsh fact is that Arlene's "big thing" is the stage more than TV.

"Television's wonderful," she says, a little wistfully, "but you get into such a routine with the commercials and the ad libs that while it's fine for sustenance, you want a little caviar once in a while, and by caviar I mean the stage.

"The audience may not think it's caviar," she added quickly and modestly when we discussed this, "but *I* think it's caviar."

Gabel—gifted actor and director that he is—explains, "To the people of my generation the greatest aspiration was the stage. The mass media—movies, radio, and TV—never came up to it. A great topper to any kind of a career was success on the Broadway stage.

"Take a girl out of a chorus line out to Hollywood," he elaborated. "Put her in a movie—protect her—let her do one line at a time over and over—and she might become known as an actress, but that's not what is really acting by our standards."

Arlene says if anyone influenced her in her early theater days, it was George Abbott.

She'd heard that "there was a part for a girl with a Spanish accent" in a show called "All That Glitters."

Having acquired a Spanish accent in a radio serial, she auditioned and Abbott quite surprisingly gave her the part.

As Arlene told me of this experience we were having lunch at Des Artistes restaurant, which she visits often at lunchtime, and she was mixing me a salad to show that she could.

I was amused at her tale of getting a Spanish accent because in mixing the salad she asked a waiter in good Bostonese for some "papriker."

It was a hard-boiled-egg salad that she was concocting, and her patter ran like this:

"You understand, of course, I don't have the right tools here. . . . I'm only doing this for you. . . . Some days [while stirring it] I can't do a thing with it. . . . Now I want a real lemon. . . . None of that canned-lemon-juice nonsense! . . . There, now, try that. . . . Well? . . . What do you mean, you're not hungry?"

Once a dozen years ago when Arlene was in the hit show "The Doughgirls," playing a Russian sniper, she maintained in an interview that she believed in leprechauns, astrology, and little people.

She'd been in seven straight flop shows and had the feeling she was a jinx to shows and that nobody wanted her. In fact, nobody did seem to want her, most emphatically, every time she looked for a job.

One day she lunched in a hotel that had a fortune teller, and wrote her question out, to wit: "When will I get my next job in the theater?"

She was almost more depressed than when she came in as he began answering her. "I see nothing for June, July, August, or September," he said.

"But watch November seventeenth."

That was the date that rehearsals for "The Doughgirls" began.

For Arlene, being a thoroughly likable person was no accident of birth and environment, though those things might have helped. She sat down as a child and planned it that way.

"My nose is too long and I'm too skinny, but maybe that won't make any difference if I'm fun to be with," she analyzed, with almost frightening objectivity. "I'm going to try to please other people."

This as an eleven-year-old girl at the Convent of Mount St. Vincent in Riverdale, N. Y., where, though not a Roman Catholic, she was sent to school.

"A major plank in my platform was 'good talk.' I knew that boys, some of the nicest, tended to be shy unless properly prodded, or inspired, and prod or inspire them I would.

"Ever since then, I've been a reader—books, newspapers, magazines, current events, of course, but never neglecting important things like baseball."

After the convent, Arlene went on to Finch's Finishing School.

Later, as a successful actress, she made the casual but flippant-sounding comment on her tenure there in an interview: "I did learn to pour tea."

And the dean of the school replied in beautiful rhetoric, "I have looked up your record and while you received an A in Psychology and a B in History and a B plus in English, I could find no mark for pouring tea."

"I apologized," said Arlene, "and I *was* sorry."

Nowadays, perhaps as a result of that lesson, her famed wit, striking as it does with authority and, sometimes, lacking in discretion, never sneers.

What likely was an accident of birth is her unquestioned vivacity, and flowing from that, her flair for acting.

The good nuns, way back then, saw this and advised her father of Arlene's suitability for the theater. Father must have realized it, too, but struggled against it, and nature, for many years before surrendering.

His carefully plotted diversionary movement—establishing Arlene as the proprietress of a Madison Avenue giftshop—was a well-played fiasco.

"I sold about a vase a month," Arlene reminisces. "Once, a Harvard man left behind his bottle of rye, and from that I made my biggest profits."

With her father's at-best reluctant consent, she safaried to Hollywood for a short-lived residency.

"Short-lived, indeed, when Dad saw a what-was-then cheesecake poster of me adorning a New York theater and wired, 'Have seen you half-naked on Broadway. Come home at once.'"

That she did, but Daddy had learned that she *would* be an actress and, eventually, came to take a father's peculiarly fierce pride in her achievements.

You don't quite know how influential Arlene is till you read some of her fan mail. In Seattle and Mayfield Heights, Ohio, and with people like a five-year-old boy named Mark, she wields power.

The influence would seem to be a healthy, beneficial one.

93

Mark's mother wrote Arlene to tell of her son's adulation for her. His every act was prefaced with a "Will Arlene like it if I eat my cereal?" sort of thing. Mark took a magazine cover with Arlene's picture to bed with him. He liked to cuddle it. "I'm afraid you have more control over him than I do," the mother wrote.

"Dear Mark," Arlene answered. "I'm glad to have a fan like you. And I wish I could be with you so I could cuddle you.

"But make the most of your cuddling time, 'cause when you get to be eight like my son, you'll probably be thinking about baseball all the time. But then when you get still older, you'll go back to thinking about cuddling again."

And she sent along a small, cuddle-sized photo, so Mark wouldn't have to tote the bulky magazine cover to bed.

A man forwarded a letter from his wife which Arlene treasures.

"I was terribly lonely for you, but I'd spend an hour with Arlene [on "Home"] and her warmth and love for people filled me with gladness."

Corny? Maybe. But not to a couple of people, and not to Arlene.

Another member of the "cult" is Muriel Fleet, Arlene's secretary, herself a warm person who believes Arlene can do anything.

She told me so.

"Arlene can do anything."

"Like what, for instance?"

"Oh, she can cook."

I couldn't contain a laugh. "So she can cook. Can't all women?" The last was a rhetorical question.

Miss Fleet rose to the challenge.

"Well, when I left, Arlene was tuning Peter's [her son] violin. And she can sing. She sings around the house and she's grand. And she can paint. She doesn't think so, but I *know* she can paint."

It would appear that Arlene's pretty good as a mother, too.

Son Peter is a bright boy who goes to Hunter College

elementary school, which is often called the "school for geniuses." He has an I.Q. of 135-140. "He is," Miss Fleet remarks fondly but in mock horror, "disgustingly well-adjusted."

The boy has shown symptoms of being a congenital wit.

He bragged to Muriel of his air travel. "I've been to New York and Chicago and I flew *back* from California."

"Did you go to California by car?" Miss Fleet asked.

"No."

"By train?"

"No."

"Well, Peter, how *did* you get there?"

"I was born there."

Arlene and Peter breakfast together, then she drops him off at school. They're both Giant fans. And the pair occasionally form a good-looking battery on the sidewalk in front of their East Side home.

In another respect, her bringing-up-Peter does her credit. She's Armenian and her parents were of the Greek-Orthodox faith. She attended a Roman Catholic convent. Her husband is Jewish.

Peter asked her one day, when two Jewish holidays were approaching, what he should do about school.

"I think," she decided with humored wisdom, "you should stay home one day for your father and go one day for me."

A considerable part of her warmth lies in the fact that she can be busy, yea hectic, but she doesn't become preoccupied.

"She's so approachable," her secretary says.

At Christmas, she buys gifts for everyone connected with her three shows, as well as her other friends. Though they number in the score, she insists on selecting them all herself.

"And we wrap them," Miss Fleet attests. "Arlene has a flair for fancy bows."

To make time for playing ball and buying gifts and taking trips, she had to give up something. Long telephone conversations are taboo.

"How, being a woman, does she do it?" I asked of her secretary.

"For one thing," Muriel replied, "she doesn't gossip. And if the other party is inclined to, well, it can get discouraging when all the response you get is 'Uh-huh' and 'Yea' and 'Oh.'"

Then, too, there's a telephone on each of the floors of her home. At the desk beside each one are a pair of glasses, a fountain pen, and scads of note paper. Arlene always carries a spare pair of glasses.

After "What's My Line?" on Sunday, Arlene and Gabel almost ritualistically go to the Herbert Bayard Swopes' on Park Avenue to the Sabbath open house where, as Arlene says, "We have supper and mix."

The Gabels and Swopes have been friends for many years, and Arlene enjoys declaiming about Mr. Swope's prodigious hospitality, alleging that one night he phoned home and said, "Maggie, there'll be forty-eight coming out to dinner tonight, and incidentally, I'll be tied up at the office and can't make it."

Lately Arlene has added public speaking to her busy life.

"She's gotten quite good at it," her husband says with some pride. "That takes work, too, for she bones up. It's kind of an education thing.

"These TV gals," he adds, "will be the best-educated people in America."

Arlene is constantly asking her husband such puzzlers as "Why is Dizzy Dean listed as Jerome Herman Dean in one biography and as Jay Hanna in another one?" Gabel, who had probably thought of Dean as "Old Diz," was surprised at the revelation that Diz had led a double life, but not surprised that Arlene had caught him red-handed.

Arlene had, on her day off, agreed to help out with Ladies' Day on Diz' TV show. She had, characteristically, boned up on her teammate, starting with the very simple problem of "What is his real name?"

Arlene is five feet six, a size ten, has brown eyes, is a blond "now." Once, though, she had a nickname: "Brownie."

She has a flair for dialects. She's done Russian and Spanish roles on the stage. She and Gabel, when they're inclined, go into a "veddy, veddy" British routine that, Miss Fleet thinks, "is hilarious."

Her "wit," that overworked word for sense of humor, is, I guess, uncontainable.

What else can you say about a gal who wired the newborn babe of a friend, "Don't take any wooden nipples."

DAVE GARROWAY'S

VITAL STATISTICS:

Born David Cunningham Garroway, Jr., Schenectady, New York; July 13, 1913. Attended University High School, St. Louis, Mo.; B.A. degree from Washington University, St. Louis, in 1935.

Married Pamela Wilde, August, 1956. Has one daughter, Paris, age thirteen, by previous marriage.

Was a Radio City page boy at $65 per month in 1938; current earnings exceed $340,000 per annum.

Attracted nationwide attention with "Garroway at Large" television program, Chicago, 1949. Became star of "Today" show, January, 1952.

Sports-car enthusiast; possessor of more than 500 bow ties.

During World War II served three years as communications officer, U.S. Navy.

EARLY BIRD CATCHES THE RATING

Dave Garroway was playing golf on the Tam o' Shanter course in Chicago one day with an opponent who was betting him $10 to $1 he wouldn't make a birdie on the hole.

Feeling suddenly confident of himself, Garroway wasn't satisfied at trying to score one under par . . . he wanted to try for two under par.

"By the way," he asked his opponent, "do I win the bet if I get an eagle?"

"No," said his opponent. "I'll give you odds of $50 to $1 that you don't get an eagle."

"I'll take $10 worth," replied Garroway, who proceeded to make the hole, almost miraculously, in two strokes, winning $500.

It would seem, from this, that David Cunningham Garroway—"Old Sobersides" or "Goggle Eyes," as he is sometimes called—just knows that he is good. And not just at golf, although he's always excelled in that. When he was a boy living in St. Louis, he and his father, David Garroway, Sr., a mechanical engineer, usually entered the father-and-son tournaments. Eventually these tournaments were abandoned.

The participants lost heart—"Garroway and son" always won.

Sometimes nowadays, Dave Garroway's morning TV competition also feels despairing. Sponsors now cry for Dave, till he can only turn them down. Steady, slow-talking, sincere-sounding old Dave's "Today" show is an NBC uranium mine. The glib, slick-tongued, high-pressure announcers who used to snatch the best jobs away from Dave—because he couldn't talk fast—have fallen by the wayside. But Dave's relaxed methods have put him at the peak of his network's profit-making pinnacle. His "Today" program was butchered to bits by some of the critics when it started January 14, 1952, but now has become a morning habit of millions of viewers, including housewives who shattered the family budgets for portable TV sets—or cut holes in the walls between their kitchen and living room so they could watch Dave on their TV set while getting breakfast. Millions of husbands were moved into the living room to have breakfast, and quit looking at their wives to look at Dave.

Dave's one-word success story seems to be: "Garroway."

"He isn't selling products when he does a commercial, he's selling Garroway," some of his associates maintain.

Dave hates to tell jokes and can't sing, dance, or emote. He's a naturally inquisitive soul who has microscopes and telescopes in his apartment, and has learned to grind his own lenses. He's a well-informed amateur astronomer. Yet his curiosity takes other turns.

"I wonder what it would be like to sit around with a beautiful girl sometime and just look at her without having to hear her talk or being forced to talk to her," Dave said one day to Charlie Andrews, for several years his only writer.

"Why don't we find out?" replied Andrews.

"Sure!" said Garroway seriously. "We'll call up a model agency."

They phoned and announced they'd like to rent a couple of pretty girls to take to lunch. There was one thing the girls must do: NOT talk. The two beauties met Garroway and Andrews in a plush restaurant.

"Hello," cooed the more forward girl.

"Now, now, no talking!" scolded Garroway.

For three or four minutes it was amusing, but then it became embarrassing. Dave and Andrews were both happy when it was over.

Garroway believes in being believable. And he believes in being "nice," that is, in being courteous and using good taste. Never a "blow-top," he may, however, get angry about something going wrong on his program—but he never yells. He goes to his dressing room, closes the door, and sits there alone, simmering, till the anger passes.

Once—and only once—did he have any trouble with an interviewee. And he behaved characteristically.

A man with a specially constructed automobile was about to set out on a trip.

"How long do you think it will take you?" Garroway inquired.

"Frankly, I don't give a damn how long it will take," the man said.

Garroway didn't say a word. He simply walked away and left the man standing there feeling terribly alone, although millions had just been looking at him. The cameras, of course, followed Garroway, and the man was not seen on camera again. Garroway was aware that children were watching the show and felt that he couldn't sanction such talk. Never has a

TV interview ended so abruptly—but some 2,400 letters informed Garroway they approved of his disapproval.

This is part of Dave's natural way of being nice. For years, when some writer or other helper has said to him, "Here's a little gimmick you could use," Dave has said, "Would it be believable?"

"How can you do something completely unbelievable as entertainment and then expect anybody to believe your commercial?" he reasons.

The result is that the six-foot-two, two-hundred-pound, horn-rimmed, bow-tied Garroway may occasionally be criticized for his entertainment, or lack of it—but the sponsors and sponsors' wives always love his commercials.

Jack Lescoulie, Dave's announcer and occasional replacement, has found that one secret of Dave's success as a salesman is his refusal to be hurried.

"You can't get him to take a speed-up signal," says Lescoulie.

"When we were starting, I used to tell him after a program, 'I was trying to signal you to speed up.'

"Dave would say, 'I know you were.'"

Jack finally got the idea . . . that Dave wasn't going to change his personality for anybody. And he hasn't yet. He feels that to speed up his pace, he would become phony, and that inasmuch as he's not a great actor, the phoniness would be detected by the viewers.

Once, however, Dave did have to hurry a commercial, somewhat.

He was having a girl sing at a soda fountain, and Charlie Andrews thought it would be amusing if Dave got his tie caught in a milk-shake mixer.

"I might get hurt," objected Dave.

"Let's try it," urged Andrews, and they did. It worked, and harmlessly. A stagehand would cut the tie with scissors just when it looked like Dave was about to be choked. But Dave's silk tie got mussed in the experiment, so Andrews took off his black knit tie and Dave put it on.

That came close to ending Garroway's career, and Garroway, too. The knit tie was of much heavier material, and the scissors wouldn't cut through it just at the crucial moment when the mixer was tightening the tie around Dave's neck. It was also time to do the commercial.

"Dave had a choice of strangling or doing a commercial with a mixer around his neck," Andrews remembers.

Gurglingly, he started the commercial, but had to take time out when firmer, heavier hands were applied to the scissors, which cut the tie and saved his neck just in time. Garroway has never criticized the stunt, though, because it surely was believable—"much too believable for comfort," he says.

When he's reminiscing and telling his success story step by step, Garroway enjoys remarking that he finished second in a class of twenty-four when he attended the NBC announcers' school.

"Second from the bottom," he explains.

"I finished twenty-third."

Dave attended this school in New York—around 1939 and 1940. He first saw the light of Schenectady, N.Y., on July 13, 1913. His father, who was of Scottish descent, was with General Electric, and the family flitted from city to city as the company ordered. Dave got out of University High School in St. Louis in 1931, majored in English at Washington University, where he was graduated in 1935—and for three months was a salesman of piston rings.

Unlikely as it seems, everybody had a piston ring, and then Dave had a brief fling at the Harvard Business School.

NBC was looking for bright young men with business background, so it gave a job to young Dave. The job: NBC page. The salary: $16 a week.

If you made an NBC tour during the 1937 or 1938 World's Fair in New York, Dave could have been the tall, spectacled "guide" who helped steer you around.

Farmed out to KDKA in Pittsburgh and then to WMAQ in Chicago, Dave was just getting started when the Navy grabbed him for three years. He came out a lieutenant senior grade in 1945 and went back to Chicago—where he would sit around in a bar brooding about the more fortunate announcers.

103

"All these other guys get the choice jobs simply because I can't talk fast enough," he would state to his beer, or his beer-drinking buddies.

"You gotta learn to punch," they'd tell him.

"I *can't* punch," he'd answer . . . and they'd shrug eloquently . . . their shrug implying that if he didn't become a high-pressure guy, he'd soon be off NBC's payroll entirely.

Dave was worrying about being divorced not only by NBC but by his wife, Adele Dwyer, whom he'd married in 1940. When they did bust up, Dave and writer Charlie Andrews began living together, and Andrews began feeding him material for a midnight radio disc-jockey program called "The 11:60 Club." Dave later married lovely Pamela Wilde.

By April, 1949, the "Garroway at Large" TV show was launched, and people began exclaiming about the "Chicago school of television"—but particularly about Garroway, who seemed so casual that viewers got the idea he was ad libbing almost everything.

The late Fred Allen was one of his first enthusiasts; another was Henry Morgan.

"Dave Garroway out in Chicago is the only one who's making the proper use of this new medium," Fred told me about this time. Allen went to Chicago to study the young man, and his methods.

Henry Morgan's face was already well known to TV fans, and he also appeared on the show, looking quite perplexed about the whole thing. Garroway walked from set to set, frequently passing Morgan, who sat on a stool, but never mentioning him or talking to him.

The show's closing line was, "This program came to you from Chicago."

After being ignored for the whole program, although on camera repeatedly, Morgan heard the punch line about the show coming from Chicago, and said his only word on the program.

"Chicago!" he exclaimed.

Dave is antiparty. He's probably glad that his curious working hours—he gets up at 4 A.M.—enable him to duck most cocktail crushes. Rather than recite the latest risqué story when he gives a dinner party, Dave's likely to enchant his guests with tales of the late Charles Fort, the inspiration for the "Fortean Society," who traced items he read or heard about, such as skies raining red frogs. Garroway's guests at a recent party were of the younger generation and had not heard about Fort, whose research entranced collectors of curios a couple of decades ago.

Frequently moody, Garroway also has a quirky sense of humor. When his "Garroway at Large" TV show was going well in Chicago, with Congoleum as the sponsor, he took the summer off to see Europe with Charlie Andrews. The world looked bright.

They'd reached Zermatt, Switzerland, the beautiful little Alpine village at the foot of the Matterhorn, which is so craggy that autos don't undertake it. Tourists ascend to the town by rail; then horse-drawn buses take them and their luggage to their inns.

Late at night, Garroway received a phone call from New York.

He didn't mention it to Andrews. But after Andrews went to bed he walked around the village most of the night, dropping in at one of the bars to hear the yodelers and to observe the mountain climbers about to start out with the dawn.

At sun-up, Garroway roused Andrews.

"Wake up. I want to show you the most beautiful sight in the world," he shouted.

Pulling back the shades, he pointed to the snowy peak of the treacherous Matterhorn in the early sun, and as Andrews drank in the view, Garroway announced in a low voice:

"Congoleum dropped the show."

Actually, the sponsor, unable to get the station coverage from NBC that had been promised, had chosen to give up TV for a while. The New York call the night before was from Garroway's late manager, "Biggie" Levine, giving him the bad news. The two travelers returned to America, somewhat disconsolate.

Dave was off TV for twenty-six weeks, although he was

paid anyway. Then began the talk about the "Today" show
—and its launching.

"Nobody'll ever know how hard he worked to make this
show go," says another intimate of Dave's, who points out
that most of the fight isn't really in the studio.

"He's probably eaten 800 lunches with advertising people
and prospective clients," this informant says.

"He's cut as high as 500 hours of film merely to be sent to
prospective clients as prospective commercials. Sometimes
these are greetings to people he can't meet."

This sort of personal attention of course is invaluable to
NBC—particularly since very few TV personalities welcome
it. Show people, especially, are loath to "get together and
talk business" with clients, since it seems somehow to grate
on their artistic natures.

Garroway's rooters say he is perhaps extremely fortunate
in that respect, since he did not come from a show-business
family.

The studio grind itself is a killing one, for there's a full-
scale rehearsal five mornings a week at five o'clock.

That means Dave must roll out of his bed on Park Avenue
at around four—which sometimes is difficult if he's had a
Broadway theater opening the night before. The opening-
night shows "break" at around ten-thirty, and after a man
battles his way out and into Sardi's for a snack, it's midnight
or later before he gets home.

But Dave often says the hours are probably harder on
his staff, especially Mary Kelly, a cheery, Boston-bred ex-
secretary who's his guest-getter-upper for people appearing
on the show, as well as an expert reporter.

The 7 A.M. starting time is extremely early for the majority
of Dave's celebrated interviewees. Dave takes no chances on
them sleeping through.

"We'll have you picked up at six o'clock," Dave—or an
assistant—informs the guest. At about 5:45 A.M., Miss Kelly
arrives in a limousine and starts hanging around the hotel
or apartment lobby acting like a loiterer. In her first days
on the job, when she wasn't known, a couple of night clerks
had their suspicions about her and notified the police. But

now she's friendly with the clerks at the better hotels and if she were to oversleep—which she's never done so far—they'd probably do the awakening for her.

Eager to get the top names when they're "hot" in the news, Dave failed once with Ava Gardner—though it wasn't Mary's fault.

"I'd hired a Cadillac to drive her the ten blocks from the Hampshire House," Mary recalled.

"But when I arrived to pick her up, I couldn't raise anybody in her suite. I went back to the studio feeling bitter.

"Two days later I found out she and Frankie'd patched up one of their long quarrels and she wasn't even in the hotel. She'd forgotten me in her bliss of being back with Frank."

Frank Lloyd Wright told Mary: "You remind me of my granddaughter, Anne Baxter."

"Oh, she's nice!" Mary said.

"She was," agreed Wright, "before she went Hollywood."

Bernarr Macfadden kept putting his arm around Mary. He insisted on walking the thirty blocks to the studio.

Mary found Gregory Ratoff waiting on a street corner for her to pick him up.

"I couldn't sleep from vurrying I vould overslept," said Ratoff.

Garroway's only "studio audience" is that curious cluster of humanity that pushes its many faces up against his NBC window each morning. One day a passerby chanced to be Harry Truman. Spotting him, Mary whooshed out, loped after him, and introduced herself.

"Oh yes, nice to see you again," smiled the ex-President, shaking hands.

Miss Kelly smiled about this, for they'd never met.

At Garroway's urging, Mary planted a hand-mike in his fist and got him to say a few words, to the satisfaction of Dave, who is still a little startled when he thinks back to the day he looked out the window and saw an ex-President staring in. Another time, ex-President Truman was taking a morning stroll accompanied by George Jessel, who was then on ABC. Probably for expediency, Jessel spoke up, "He can't go on the air for you—I'm on a rival network."

Occasionally such performers as Frank Sinatra have given Dave a passing wave from the sidewalk. Henny Youngman, the night-club comedian, thinks nothing of stopping by for a bow on his way home to Brooklyn after doing a show. Frank Lloyd Wright was so enchanted with the idea of becoming a performer that he canceled a plane passage home so he could do the 9 A.M. strip after having pleased himself with his 7 A.M. show.

"How does he get up at four o'clock?" Dave's friends often wonder. At 3:45 A.M. his clock-radio turns the radio on, and gives him a few powerful nudges. At 4 A.M. an alarm clock finishes the job of waking him.

"Actually, I have a lot of time; I can slop around till four-fifteen," says Dave, who takes no special credit for such hours.

"Everybody on our show gets four or five hours sleep;" he says. "You can do it if you have a motive, such as getting up to do a show. But I can't do it on Saturday, my day off, when I don't have the motive."

Physicians who have given Dave regular checkups found him in good shape despite a four-hour sleeping average. "I think I ought to be growing some kind of ulcers, but I don't seem to be able to," says Garroway.

His odd hours have brought him some quaint experiences. Once in a while, Garroway walks to work, and one morning as he was hastening along in the dawn, he was accosted by a man whom he remembers as "pleasantly drunk." Fixing a bloodshot eye on Dave, the drunk said, "You look like Dave Garroway to me, and I hate to tell you this, but you better get home and get some sleep because you gotta a show pretty soon."

"I didn't have the heart to tell him," says Dave, "that I was already on the way to work."

Personally disinterested in drinking, Garroway has been known to pour some bourbon and scotch into one glass, and add a little wine, then down the whole mess.

"People who mix their drinks in an evening do the same thing," he explains. "I just do it faster and more efficiently." It doesn't seem to hurt or even shake his big-shouldered frame. On trips he may be seen taking a swig from a bottle that he pulls from a brown paper sack. There's nothing illegal or illicit about this. It's a vitamin-deficiency medicine prescribed by physicians.

Ad-agencyites sometimes refer to Dave as "No-Funny-Hats Garroway," because he has an aversion to prankishness. He enjoys the reputation.

"When I tell a joke, I work so hard at making it believable that it sounds true, and just lies there," he says. "Charlie Andrews says all my jokes sound perfectly sensible, which is disastrous to jokes."

Yet he concocts many a humorous device for his program. When Walter Slezak, then starring in "Fanny," wanted to be on his show but thought it impossible because he was in bed at that hour, it was decided to bring him on the air in bed, wearing the same ballooning nightshirt he wore on the stage. Slezak's interview in bed, with Garroway demonstrating his bedside manner, was one of Garroway's funniest.

"Slezak is the kind of fellow who looks good in bed," Dave observed, and Slezak added, "I look better in bed than out of it."

"I figure," says Garroway, in trying to explain his passion for reality, "that you can't lie very much on television because the audience will soon see through you.

"The strength of that box is that it transmits character. Somehow the real person eventually comes through, no matter how good an actor he is."

So Garroway declined to take on a corn-plaster company as one of his sponsors, because he just couldn't work up any sincerity about corn plasters.

"We've literally sold everything from Cadillacs to pizza pies," Garroway says. A one-minute spot on "Today" costs more than $6,000, and a sponsor can purchase time for an entire year or for only one day. Dave, having so many interests, from the mechanical to the musical, finds it easy to get all wrapped up in the assorted products he's huckstering . . . even sewing machines, for example. In one year, Dave has no less than 150 sponsors.

Each sponsor likes personal attention, which is another

reason Garroway's usually at his office on the second floor of the RCA Building till six P.M.

One sponsor has set a record for the intimacy of its relationship with its star TV salesman. The Wright Silver Cream Company, of Keene, New Hampshire, silver-polish manufacturers, invariably come to the studio to witness Dave's delivery of their commercial in person. "They never interfere or get in anybody's way," says Dave. "Once when we took the show to Detroit, I was flattered to see that the Wrights had come along with us out there."

Characteristically, when Dave speaks of the future, he hopes that "if the TV thing ever blows over, I'll get a little garage where I can actually work on cars."

When he was still in Chicago, he had an eight-car garage with six cars, which he could rebuild or tear down for amusement.

"It's entirely a hobby and not even a deductible hobby," he says. In New York he retains his 1937 Jaguar, with a '56 Jaguar XK 140 engine, which he has raced at Palm Beach, Watkins Glen, and elsewhere, and also has a new Thunderbird, and now has attained the luxury of his own garage.

"In New York it costs more to room a car than a person," Garroway often points out.

His old Jaguar carried him to a fourth place in one race and a sixth in another, and he's done 130 m.p.h. on a straightaway. In his heart, Dave probably wishes he were a speed driver—or a mechanic. I was with Garroway on a junket to Venice for the premiere of the Katharine Hepburn picture "Summertime," when the champion driver, Bill Vukovich, was killed in the Indianapolis races.

"I guess I'll give up racing—again," sighed Garroway when he finished reading the stories in the European papers. He mentioned that the champion driver of Europe, Alberto Ascari of Italy, had been killed the week before.

"Anybody who drives that fast is asking for it," spoke up his attractive brunette wife-to-be Pamela Wilde.

Dave didn't reply.

NBC doesn't like the idea of its moneymaker dare-deviling

110

around the race tracks but hasn't put any clauses in his contract forbidding him from racing. He has little time for such amusements now, anyway. The only auto accident he's had was not in a race but while he was doing a commercial for Pontiac, then sponsor of a Garroway nighttime show, in October, 1954, at Key Biscayne, around Miami, Fla. Dave was driving and being very careful, because a photographer lay on the floor of the car grinding pictures of Dave. Garroway went through a stop sign, and the car was clobbered by a truck. "It was my fault and I got a little cut on my face out of it," he says.

Though Garroway sees the "Today" format good for him for "five, six, or seven years," he'd also like to undertake another night show—maybe a "big reality show, a musical-variety-talk program." If it takes as much effort as most big night shows take, Dave might be moving his waking hour up from 3:45 A.M. to 2:45 A.M.

"I'm happier working than not, anyway," he confesses.

As he looks back, Dave can see that he has steered much of his own course. He was back from Switzerland and off TV when he read in *Variety* of plans for the "Today" program— and he immediately decided that there was a spot for Garroway.

"I got my agent to make a pitch for it, and I auditioned," he says. "I went looking for that one real hard. I guess it was the only job I really ever went looking for."

Then came the critics' blasts. "For a whole year," he says, "it looked like I was out of my head."

Dave isn't peeved at any of the critics. In the beginning the show was a little pompous. It used expressions like "communications center of the universe," and "nerve center of the world," and Dave was called "the communicator." They eventually loosened up.

For a while, Dave was also wordy in a weird, cultural way. A new song might be "an incandescent, gossamer bit of esoteric delight," while at the same time Dave addressed a wide variety of persons as "Old Tiger."

"The 'Old Tiger' thing started with a girl I was in love with

111

in Hawaii," he admits now. "She was so much like a tiger I couldn't call her anything else."

Dave had carried these attention-attracting devices over from radio, but he soon found they didn't fit into TV. "Slowly I worked my way out of them," he says. "Anybody who criticized me for those things then was probably right."

Pat Weaver, when president of NBC, greatly admired Garroway for his variety of interests. Dave majored in Fine Arts, Abnormal Psychology, and English at Washington University, St. Louis, after finishing University City High School there—and remembers himself as being a boy who liked to go to school.

"I was a good but not extraordinary student," he maintains. "I loved to know facts.

"I'm still like that. I've been called encyclopedic. Well, that's all right, because I still read the encyclopedia. It's good reading."

Dave, another only child who made good, seems a little distant to most people meeting him the first time. He never gushes, and expects friends to feel that he likes them, rather than having to tell them. He is, like many suddenly celebrated TV stars, often embarrassed by his fame. One night his presence in a Long Island bar started a fist fight between two drunks as to whether he was Garroway. He left before the fight was over and thus never found out, as a friend put it, "whether he was or wasn't Garroway."

On his visit to Venice, where he worked quite hard filming shots around the Grand Canal and interviewing guests who arrived at the movie premiere by gondola, Garroway relaxed afterward by going to San Marco Square for a drink. At a table not far away an American said, "Mister, I'd like to buy you a drink. You happen to look a lot like an American on television named Dave Garroway. It's impossible for you to be Garroway, but I'd like to buy you a drink, anyway."

One thing that endears Garroway to thinking people is that he is living proof that TV need not be for morons. Dave is probably the only TV luminary on any network who belongs to the American Association of Variable Star Observers, which Dave characterizes as "a bunch of astronomy fans."

Dave, for example, is assigned a star to watch—known to astronomers as 61 Cygni, the "Swan."

"I make a report on its brightness," Garroway'll tell you. "But I don't need a telescope for it, though I have one—for it's a 'naked-eye' star."

"Doesn't that interfere with your very little sleep?" I asked.

"I can manage it, and besides, it's not seen again until September," he told me one June afternoon. "I'm off duty now, so to speak."

Dave purports that his reputation as a star-gazer is pretty phony, and that his only background was unlocking the doors of the Harvard Observatory laboratories and waiting while students did their work with the telescope.

"I had the title of fourth assistant laboratory instructor, which meant that I turned the key in the lock," he says.

It should be made clear here that Garroway does have many average-man traits despite his star-gazing and encyclopedia-reading. He remembers that as a student in junior high at University City, Mo., he was suspended for shooting craps in the principal's office. With the principal? Not at all. Dave's always figured that's why he was suspended.

STEVE ALLEN'S

VITAL STATISTICS:

Born December 26, 1921, in New York City, only child of "Belle Montrose and Billy Allen," well-known vaudeville team. By coincidence —after living all over the U.S.—he began his network TV career in New York City December 25, 1950.

Educated in Hyde Park High, Chicago, and Central High, Phoenix; one year Drake University, Des Moines, on journalism scholarship; part of another year, Arizona State Teachers, Phoenix.

Full name, Stephen Valentine Patrick William Allen. Reared a Catholic. Married Dorothy Goodman, Arizona State co-ed, while in college, with whom he had three sons, Stephen, Brian, and David. Divorced, 1951. Married Jayne Meadows, movie, stage, and TV actress, 1954.

Height, six feet two; weight, 195 pounds. Author of four books, *Bop Fables, The Funny Men, Fourteen for Tonight* and *Wry on the Rocks*. Nickname, "Steve-o."

SHY BOY MAKES GOOD

Steve Allen was handed a check for $10,000 for a couple of extra acting chores one afternoon recently by his manager, Jules Green.

The six-foot-two, spectacled, teacherish-looking Steve looked up from his desk in the Hudson Theater on West Forty-fourth Street in New York—and began laughing.

"What's so funny about $10,000?" asked Green, who, being a manager, holds money in high regard.

"You know," replied Allen, with the embarrassed laugh that's familiar to millions, "I'm not worth that much money."

"I know what you mean," returned Green. "I can remember the $90-a-week days and they weren't very long ago."

Steve, a comedian by profession but a poet and philosopher in private life, stared off into space and said, "But that's the way it is, isn't it?"

That was before Steve became NBC's big Sunday-night hope against Ed Sullivan. The money is much bigger now.

But he had good cause to reflect. For although only thirty-five, this introverted only child of a vaudeville team, whose boyhood was saddened by asthma—and the fact that he was a "poor kid"—was proving that a really shy guy can get rich on television.

Studious Steve's good for a half-million a year now that he's become a movie as well as TV star. At Universal in Hollywood, he starred in the life story of Benny Goodman, whom he slightly resembles—if he lifts a clarinet to his lips. His "Tonight" show on NBC—one hour and forty minutes, three and five nights a week—was almost as popular with American white-collar workers as the coffee break, because Steve's so ad glibby. Yet Steve actually reddens when asked for his autograph. Boringly bookish to some of his actor friends, Steve writes short stories, songs, and poems . . . not only that, he sells them . . . even the poems. He gets $70-a-week

116

pocket money from two corporations that are marketing his various talents. Can anybody tell Steve how a man can get rid of $70 a week? Steve's never been able to squander that much.

Not long ago, "Steve-o"—as the cast calls him—told his radiant, red-haired wife, Jayne Meadows, "I'm afraid I've lost something."

"I hope it wasn't a sponsor," said Jayne, a panelist on "I've Got a Secret."

"It was three checks I've been carrying around," he confessed.

Obviously, Steve's indifferent to money now, even though he brooded about the lack of it after his father died, when Steve was about two. The way things are going, Steve'll probably have enough by his fortieth birthday to retire. Not that he will. He can't even take vacations. They're boring.

But the story of Steve is how he became a comedian the hard, unusual way—by being bashful instead of brash. And so if you're shy, nervous, terrified of making speeches . . . well, then, let Allen be your inspiration. He's more bashful than you are. Steve is two men. He's chatty and sparkling when he comes into your living room on television, but if he came into your living room *in person*, you'd have to do most of the talking.

And even in his own living room—well, I've been there! He drove my wife and me up to his Park Avenue apartment one night after a show on which he'd been unusually scintillating. He parked his Packard and led us upstairs, where we discussed his reputation of being "the most relaxed man on television."

"Relaxed!" exclaimed my wife afterward. "Steve's a phony. He's a bundle of nerves. Did you notice how he drummed on the chair with his fingers and kept spinning his thumbs?"

"He was nervous because he was being interviewed," pointed out his manager.

"But he interviews twenty or thirty people a show," I said.

"This was *him* being interviewed," laughed Green.

Mrs. Allen confirms that Steve is genuinely shy—a man

117

with no small talk for strangers—when off the air, but getting over it.

Her sister, Audrey Meadows, who became the "Alice" of the Jackie Gleason program, introduced her to Steve in 1953 in Audrey's dressing room at "Top Banana." A party of five went afterward to the Park Sheraton Mermaid Room—and Jayne and Steve were the "unattached extras."

"Steve kept looking at the menu or the table or his hands," Jayne remembers. "I finally said to him, 'I hope you don't mind me analyzing you. But you're either painfully shy, or terribly rude.'"

Steve managed to tell her.

When the party was about to proceed to Longchamps for supper, Steve took Audrey aside. "Ask your sister to come along," he said.

"You ask her," Audrey answered.

Steve did, with some difficulty. Jayne accepted. "Ride in the front seat with me," Steve suggested.

"It was like a high-school date," Jayne recalls. From that minute on, Steve was in the hands of an amateur psychiatrist. Jayne worked one year as an assistant kindergarten teacher in Sarasota, Fla., and is fascinated at the ability of teachers to get children to be neat—not by telling them they're sloppy, but by mentioning how well they look when they comb their hair. It's known as the "positive approach."

Probably Jayne was anxious to try out the kindergarten method on Steve. When one girl in the party was going to take a taxi home to Brooklyn that first night, Jayne spoke up: "Oh, no, we've got a car. We'll drive you home."

"I got a chance to talk to this man for an hour," Jayne says.

The result was that Jayne told Audrey a few days later, "Steve asked me for a date."

"Where are you going? To El Morocco?" asked Audrey.

"To the Planetarium," shrugged Jayne.

"The Planetarium!" howled Audrey. To herself, she said, "Well, that's the end of this boy."

Jayne found the Planetarium enchantingly romantic, and Night Court, where they went on another date, equally engrossing. Jayne feels that it took a gabby gal like herself to get Steve to loosen up conversationally. He's made a lot of progress, and one of these days, she promises, "he'll be talking up a tornado."

Stephen Valentine Patrick William Allen has battled this shyness since childhood—and it's been particularly excruciating because he's always wanted to be an actor.

To visit him backstage and watch him work is to see "the other Steve," the glib one who's fearless before a microphone or a camera. Moving through the studio audience with a portable mike on the old "Tonight" show, he was a well of wit.

An undertaker was in the audience one night when I was there. "Are you here on business or pleasure?" Steve asked him.

"Why did I have to wait outside for an hour tonight?" another man wanted to know. "I guess it's because you got here an hour early," Steve told him.

A music student was next. "What kind of music are you studying?" Steve inquired.

"I'm studying pop," the student said.

"Is your mother under observation, too?" asked Steve.

A chemistry professor sitting near me didn't bother Steve. "A chemistry professor?" Steve said. "What do you chem?" Steve then asked the professor what he thought of chemistry sets for boys. The professor thought they were all right.

"That shows what you know about it," shot back Steve. "My son got one and blew up the apartment with it." He quickly added, "I'm only kidding."

Steve shoved the mike toward a man named Matt Russo and asked him his occupation.

"I'm a TV actor when I can get some work. I'm also a truck driver," Russo confessed.

"Hmm." Steve emitted his nervous chuckle. Handing Russo a gift—one of thousands that were sent to Steve by manufacturers and distributors hoping for a free mention—he asked Russo, "Is that a robe or a smoking jacket, Matt?"

"It's a robe, Steve." Russo proudly held it up.

"It's a smoking jacket, Matt, and I'll get a bucket of water and put it out," Steve said.

Regardless of how they look on paper, they were funny to many millions of TV viewers. A woman in Winston-Salem, N.C., who told me, "I stay up so late watching Steve Allen that I can't get up early enough to watch Arthur Godfrey," echoed the lament uttered then by many, many housewives. Unfunny as he looks, Steve can make people laugh just by the way he handles words. He has a great facility for making jokes by taking the "wrong meaning" of a word, or a sentence, as was just illustrated. He also has a quick eye and ear for the ludicrous.

"Here," a man in the audience told him one night, "are two tickets to a show."

"Thanks," answered Steve, "I'll both go."

But at times his insecurity shows itself, as it did one night when a woman called up to him, "I have an orange I want to give you."

"Well, why don't you just throw it up here?" Steve called back. "No, on second thought, you'd better not. It might start a trend."

Steve's bashful battle to become an actor was a natural one, for he made his show-business début before he was a year old.

His mother, Belle Donohue, an acrobat with a sense of humor, adopted the stage name of Montrose, married song-and-dance man Billy Allen, and they teamed as "Montrose and Allen." Steve was born in New York the day after Christmas, 1921, and was on the stage quickly thereafter.

"They often dragged out a tiny basket when they did a version of 'The Volga Boatman,' and I'm told that now and then I was in the tiny basket," says Steve.

Steve's struggle commenced with his father's death. His mother returned to Chicago, her home town, and they lived with "Aunt Margaret" Donohue, a spinster who worked at the American Railway Express Company. Young Stephen was reared all the way from Johnstown, Pa., to San Francisco, mainly with the help of loquacious Irish aunts. When he was seven, he spent a summer in Allentown, Pa.

"One of my aunts hit a daily double and went to Pennsylvania to visit one of my uncles," Steve says.

It seemed to Steve, who had a sad, dreamy, skinny look, that he was always moving and was always the "new kid." He thought his asthma and glasses made him unattractive. "I'm so nearsighted I have to wear contact lenses to see my glasses," he says now.

Young Stephen had to win over each new group with jokes. He learned the value of humor early.

Steve's remembered by a former teacher of his, Margaret Byrne, as being a "twentieth-century Shakespeare" at Hyde Park High in '39 and '40. Cutting a math class, he'd sit on a bench in Jackson Park writing verse for an English class. He was frequently suspended from school for ducking the duller classes—but due to a conspiracy between students and Miss Byrne, he was able to get smuggled into the English class.

"The other pupils liked him so much they would form a human screen around him so nobody from the principal's office could see him come into class," Miss Byrne says now—not denying that she helped a little.

Just for practice, Steve would knock off a composition—or even a sonnet—for a fellow student. Miss Byrne recalls a girl student ripping her paper out of a typewriter after hearing one of Steve's compositions read. "And I thought I could write!" she groaned.

Steve wore literary-type sideburns and had a gal to whom he wrote a sonnet titled, "A Girl Smiled." This poem, by the way, is in his book "A Pocketful of Wry" (Henry Holt). His verses began appearing in the Chicago *Tribune's* celebrated "A Line o' Type or Two" column.

As he didn't get paid for these, Steve didn't impress his mother, who told him he was "shiftless."

When he was sixteen, Steve came home and announced, "I won $100 tonight!"

"How?" demanded his short, roundish little mother, suspecting a crap game.

"For first prize in an essay contest." Steve'd written on "Rediscovering America" in a contest run by the Civitan organization. His mother began taking a new view of his writing ambitions.

Appointed editor of the school literary magazine, *Pens*, Steve dashed off a show to raise money for it. One song went like this:

"It all depends
On whether you buy *Pens*."

Music came as easy as writing, and he made two or three dollars a night as pianist for small neighborhood bands. The literary lion of Hyde Park High next took notice of Garry Moore—only seven years his senior—who was then in his early twenties and starting a Chicago radio show.

After many days of effort, Steve took a neatly bound, personally illustrated volume of his jokes and poems to Moore—hoping to land a job as a gag writer.

"A little immature but you have talent," said Moore. "Would you leave your name?"

Steve left his name and—he found out when he got home—also his precious book. In his nervousness, he'd forgotten to pick it up and maybe it wound up in some wastebasket. Steve never saw this genuine first edition of the *Collected Works of Steve Allen* again.

Some authorities consider asthma's due to emotional upset. Regardless, Steve, when poor, had it; comfortably fixed, he doesn't.

"It only kicks up now," he says, "if I'm around cigars or dogs. What would *really* bother me would be a dog smoking a cigar."

Young Steve was sent to Phoenix for his asthma. A teacher came into the office of the high-school paper one day and asked, "Any of you kids want a journalism scholarship at Drake University?"

Steve grabbed it—after the other seniors said they'd picked their colleges—because he had no money for tuition.

He hankered to be a reporter during his year at the Des Moines university. But with the scholarship used up, he entered Arizona State Teachers College, back in Phoenix. He's a researcher, a prober, a peerer-into-musty-volumes, in his quiet hours, and he thought seriously of switching to the sedate life of a pedagogue.

"But I had to make some money," Steve says. "Radio announcing looked like the easiest way.

"An announcer doesn't have to have any brains. He just needs a throat. There are announcers who are smart. But they don't have to be."

Steve got a $45-a-week job as staff announcer at Station KOY in Phoenix. He also soon got a wife—Dorothy Goodman, an attractive Phoenix girl. Then he was hired—at $90 a week —to play piano in a steak joint. He couldn't read music, and can't today, though he's written over a thousand songs.

The wealth was rolling in and piling up. When he'd saved a thousand dollars, Steve took his bride and their small son to Los Angeles to try to crash the Big Time.

He crowded the family of three into one rented room. He went looking for work around the networks. He didn't find any. His money got low.

At CBS, Steve found an old friend from Phoenix who said, "I can't hire you—but you can use my office and my typewriter."

From there, Steve submitted ideas for programs, as well as jokes to working comedians. Too embarrassed to admit he couldn't find a job, Steve gave his wife the impression that he was working "for the man down at CBS."

"When's he going to pay you?" his wife asked Steve after several weeks of this.

"I'm afraid to ask him. He might fire me," Steve said.

Just when bankruptcy loomed, Steve was offered three jobs in one week. He became a staff announcer at KFAC. Steve Allen was at that moment launched as a comedian. Nobody else—least of all KFAC—knew it, but Steve was sure of it.

"When I was sure nobody else was listening—from midnight to four A.M.—I'd tell jokes," Steve will tell you now, in a stealthy whisper.

The joke—and jokes—were on Steve in his first real attempt to be a comic. His show was dropped.

He'd switched from KFAC to KMTR for a few dollars more a week—so somebody must have been listening to the late-night jokes. At KMTR he and another announcer, Wendell Noble, would sit around grousing about the station's comedians and boasting how much better they could do.

They got their chance in a show called "Smile Time," a program starring them, "two announcers with a sense of humor."

"For two years," says Steve, "I wrote a fifteen-page comedy script every day. I started by rewriting the old joke books. Then I decided to try to get some humor out of something besides the written jokes."

When "Smile Time" finally left Mutual officials unsmiling, they canceled it, greatly deflating the two would-be funny men.

CBS offered Steve a late disc-jockey show. "I took it in order to eat," says Steve, "but I thought it was a comedown."

Steve soon saw that here he had an opportunity to resume his battle to become a comedian. As soon as possible, he quit playing records on his record show and sneaked in an audience to laugh at his jokes.

Thus was born—on radio—the "Steve Allen Show" as it is today.

He just kidded around, played the piano, and talked to people. Al Jolson, Groucho Marx, or Herbert Marshall might phone and say, "Can I come down tonight?" In a few weeks he had a surprising following. He was given a chance on television—broadcasting wrestling matches.

"He's got a hammerlock on him, but I think it's illegal," Steve said at one match. "He's using a real hammer."

In late '49 and early '50, when Steve was only twenty-eight,

CBS Vice-President Harry Ackerman began telling the New York office that Steve would be a sure hit on TV in New York. There was no coaxial cable yet—to be important in television, you had to be in Chicago or New York.

New York had its own problems and resisted. Finally, on Christmas Day, 1950, Steve started on TV from New York—but he wasn't happy about it.

For this night owl was trying to be funny afternoons.

"I'm not the afternoon type," Steve contends. "I do better with night-crawlers like myself. I was also working in front of a lot of women who were mad at me because Tom Breneman was dead. They didn't want any young whippersnapper trying to take his place."

But Steve's off-beat methods attracted attention. Steve feels that a show's better when something goes wrong. And since it's seldom that everything goes right in television, he has nothing to worry about. On one early show, a fly buzzed around Steve's face. It might have distracted another comedian.

"Put the camera on that fly," Steve suggested. "Let everybody see what a fly looks like."

Viewers were fascinated. Steve named the fly Floyd.

"We had Floyd the Fly making return engagements for a couple of weeks," Steve remembers. "He was the best and cheapest guest star we ever had. All we had to pay him was his board."

But Steve was sad. He and Dorothy Goodman were now parents of three sons—but their marriage was breaking up. Steve's a very moral man, and this hurt him deeply. His show was still on sustaining, and he wasn't making any progress in his campaign to get a night program. CBS couldn't persuade its affiliates to give up their cheap old movies at night to take a chance on a comedian.

"Sometimes I was so depressed when I left the stage after doing the program," Steve has since said, "I wished I could go back on camera and tell jokes instead of go out and face reality."

It was literally true that at this period, Steve's best friend was his microphone. Perhaps that's why he's so comfortable and relaxed with it now.

He was also learning that if you stick a microphone in front of somebody's mouth, something fairly interesting will come out, about nine times out of ten.

"Sometimes," as Steve himself explains this curious truth, "I will say to a man, 'Where are you from?'

"The man gets flustered and says 'Harry Simpson.'

"So I say 'Harry Simpson? Let's see, isn't that up near Boston someplace?' The man gets more nervous and says something else silly. The writers could work all day and not come up with anything funnier than that."

Everybody at CBS had tried—but eventually CBS gave up on the "Steve Allen Show," which it had launched with such high hopes. Steve went back on radio. CBS also put him on "Songs for Sale" and made him a panelist on "What's My Line?"—where he was well paid—but Steve thought that he had flopped in his first try at being a major TV comedian.

He was particularly gloomy because the world had never had a chance to see what Steve Allen could do with the night-owl crowd. He was also determined that it should have that chance.

"What you should do, Steve," Jayne Meadows told him about this time—they had just met—"is get into a Broadway comedy. You might find yourself."

Having always fancied himself an actor as well as a comedian, Steve liked the idea. He went into "Pink Elephant," which was a white one, running only four nights.

Steve had a typewriter in his dressing room, pounding out new lines for himself as well as fresh jokes for the other performers. The only good thing the critics could detect in the show was Steve. That gave him a little lift during one of his darkest periods. He got many offers to act in other plays afterward.

One day in 1953, an NBC official took notice of Steve's comparative unemployment and tried to lure him onto NBC radio.

Steve countered with the suggestion that he do a night TV show. "Dave Garroway's doing 'Today,'" mentioned Steve. "How about me doing 'Tonight'?"

The timing was perfect. NBC was able to clear time on affiliate stations. Launched locally on July 27, 1953, to run from 11:20 P.M. to midnight, the show was soon expanded to run from 11:15 P.M. to 1 A.M. in New York, and on the network from 11:30 to 1 A.M. Its success was startling, particularly to CBS, which wouldn't or couldn't give him such a time slot.

In less than six months, Steve's problem changed from "how to make some money" to "how to keep some money."

For the program alone, he received well over a quarter of a million a year, and the opportunities for sideline earnings were fantastic.

Yet to Steve, one of the big, exciting moments of his recent career was the arrival of proofs of his first accepted short story, for which he received less than $1,000. Titled "The Public Hating," this story hadn't a funny line in it. It looked ahead to 1978, when 65,000 people had come to Yankee Stadium to turn their hate on a professor convicted of a political crime.

By concentrating their hate on him—with the help of fervid appeals from a clergyman and public officials—the crowd was able to burn his flesh from his bones, according to the story. Steve wrote this story after much nighttime brooding about mind-over-matter and his fan mail, which reveals, he says, that "this is a time of umbrage-taking," when a lot of people like to hate something because there's no big war going on to use up their venom.

Steve's efforts to play reporter at New York's "Robles killing" were much more Steve Allenish.

"They just trapped Robles!" his wife, Jayne—they were married in the fall of '54—exclaimed late one afternoon as she was about to take off for a beauty parlor. "Want to go up there and see what's happening?"

Steve hopped into the car with her and was one of the first to arrive at the house, some thirty-five or forty blocks away, where police had finally cornered the mad-dog criminal. Robles was killed a few minutes later.

Pulling his hat down, and twirling his Polaroid camera—the gift of one of his sponsors—Steve mumbled, "NBC Press," and got through police lines. A couple of reporters recognized him and said "Follow us."

Some debris being flung out the windows after the gun battle just missed Steve as he started up a fire escape. A woman in an apartment adjoining the murder scene allowed Steve and his companions to grope their way through. When the police saw Steve with his Polaroid camera, they said, "You can get your pictures as soon as we've finished ours."

"It'll only take me a minute," gulped Steve, who suddenly realized that he didn't have any flash bulbs.

"I took a picture because I had a camera, which is as good a reason as I know for taking a picture," Steve says now. "The wonderful thing about the Polaroid was that it only took me a minute to find out I had a lousy picture. I didn't have to wait for several days to find out. In one way, though, it was a good picture. It looked exactly like the room did—dark."

By this time, Steve had just about completed the Horatio Alger bit and become a major comedian against terrifying odds—but a couple of wee skirmishes remained.

One was a hop to Hollywood to handle a plum assignment: M.C. of NBC's Emmy Awards dinner telecast in the whirly-girly Moulin Rouge café.

Characteristically, Steve departed on camera. About midnight he announced to his studio audience, "I'm leaving this stage in about ten minutes—DON'T APPLAUD!"

He rushed to Idlewild. Just before 1 A.M., he was at a plane ramp, mike in hand.

From then on, things were a little rough. Steve chatted with Jack Benny and producer Mike Todd, who happened to be going aboard, then greeted Gene Raymond, the actor husband of Jeanette MacDonald.

"Where's my wife—has she gone to bed?" Steve asked Raymond, who seemed surprised at the question, and then looked blank.

"Well," Raymond finally said, "I'll go up and keep her company," and trotted up the steps!

Jayne saved the situation by appearing on camera. A minute later when one passenger hurried, head down, right past Steve, rather brusquely, Steve looked into the camera and said to his audience, "You remember Adolf Hitler."

"Poor Steve must be upset," commented a woman sitting beside me.

On "Emmy Night," Steve was far more agitated—because just before show time, the public-address system in the sprawling Moulin Rouge was found to be dead.

Out there sat hundreds of dining-and-drinking guests who were supposed to roar at Steve's carefully prepared hilarities.

They couldn't even hear him when he came out to greet them.

So they ordered more booze.

"Steve was back home in California . . . and he was going to be loused up good from coast to coast," says his manager. "It was the first time I've ever seen him in real trouble."

While the seconds ticked closer and Steve floundered there flirting with disaster and maybe oblivion, Jules Green stalked up on stage and led Steve off.

It was a momentous move. The sound system was quickly fixed. The guests quieted . . . well, anyway, comparatively.

And so as the big show went on camera across the country, Steve was heard saying, "I came up here to get laughs. Now I'm willing to settle for respect." The audience roared. The sincere touch helped, too.

"You probably wonder why I'm the M.C.," Steve said. "Well, they had to get somebody who wasn't scheduled to get an award, and that left me and Pinky Lee."

They laughed again—and Steve was home. And he was in fast company. For when he saluted George Burns with, "Well, here we are—Burns and Allen," Burns cracked right back:

"Yeah, and if the other Allen were here, we'd already be getting screams!"

Steve came out a little better than the others in the madhouse.

Steve's other "test" was at the big Friars dinner for Martin and Lewis at the Waldorf, with thirty male stars—and Marilyn Monroe—on the dais.

Flashing on in a red dinner jacket, Steve said, "Fellow intellectuals, I want to apologize to you for the way I'm dressed, but I just came from a funeral."

He hoped, he said, his words of praise for the guests of honor would be fitting, but if they weren't, it was the fault of a garbled invitation. He had prepared a speech lauding another Martin and Lewis—Mary and John L.

Steve didn't "warm up the room" like Bob Hope does . . . he didn't stomp and roar and gesticulate . . . but to many he was, in his self-effacing way, the slickest thing at the dinner —next to Marilyn Monroe, of course.

On June 24, 1956, the first Steve Allen Sunday-night variety show took place, eventually necessitating curtailment of Steve on the "Tonight" show. Quick success in making himself a serious threat to Ed Sullivan caused NBC to get enthusiastic. Steve, however, remained calm about it.

He has topped Sullivan on numerous occasions. "But I just don't think Ed ever will have too much to worry about," Steve says.

Despite his modesty, ratings for the Steve Allen variety shows have been far better than NBC has enjoyed in the eight-to-nine Sunday spot for quite a while.

Sometimes a successful man's biggest battle is to remain successful after his novelty's worn off. That's Steve's new struggle. Only thirty-four at the time of his projection into "The Battle of Sunday Night," the question remains, can he keep people interested in him till he's fifty . . . or forty-five . . . or even thirty-nine, Jack Benny's age?

Steve requires nine or ten hours of sleep. "When I don't get that much my ad libs get pretty dull," Steve says.

His rise to the high places hasn't reduced Steve's ease or caused him to tread with trepidation. When I saw him at his studio just as he was ending his "Tonight" stint, I was more nervous than he.

"I'd better get out of your way—you've got a program to do," I said, rather anxiously worrying about the poor fellow.

"Stick around!" He was leisurely opening boxes at his desk on stage. "I haven't a thing to do but comb my hair.

"I can get more fun opening boxes than from jokes," he told me. From Mexico City he once received a can of "fried Agave worms," a delicacy resembling horned caterpillars. Gene Rayburn smacked his lips over them, and was designated official food-taster, worms section.

While I fretted about Steve getting on the air, a nervous party rushed up and asked Steve, "How about the hotfoot?"

Steve said to me, "I purport to have received a letter from a woman saying 'I'm tired of watching your hands all the time while you play the piano.' So we're going to do a series of unrelated pictures, mostly showing what my feet do while I'm playing the piano. In one of them my feet're getting a hotfoot."

Steve looked down at the floor and said to the nervous party, "Don't worry, I've got my hotfoot shoes on."

These are the "crazy shots" so adored by Steve Allen fans. In one of the craziest of the crazy, Steve had his crew turn a camera on the window of a near-by hotel, where a man was beating the stuffings out of a woman.

"Stuffings" was right, too—for it was a trick, and the "woman" was a dummy.

Steve now led me up to his dressing room, rubbed some liquid tonic into his wealth of black hair, and combed it carefully into a sort of an outsweep. He daubed on a little make-up. Jayne has convinced him lately that he's nice-looking, especially when he smiles.

"Well, that's all there is to it," Steve said. I tried to speed him up when he started downstairs, but he wouldn't be hastened. We came to a cot where Skitch Henderson, his orchestra leader, was stretched out with his eyes closed.

"This certainly is a nervous cast," Steve laughed.

One of Steve's perpetual problems was keeping his peculiar "Tonight" guests in line. He never let his audience get cruel toward somebody he was interviewing. One frequent guest pronounced his name in verse, like this:

"Ben Belafonte, thuh,
Rhym-ing Invent-uh."

Ben's inventions were as off-beat as Steve. They included a "genuine baseball fan"—a fan shaped like a baseball. Ben also created the "hanky-panty gag bag," which was a bag shaped like women's panties. You could reach down into this bag and draw forth assorted objects. Ben Belafonte, thuh . . . Rhym-ing Invent-uh . . . was, however, extremely logical when not around Steve. Maybe Steve did something to him.

"Helen, the world's champion bag-wood chopper," was one of his toughest guests.

"Do you chop wood in a bag?" Steve asked her.

"I chop bags of wood," Helen replied simply.

"Go ahead—only thirty chopping days till Christmas," said Steve. Helen preferred, however, to demonstrate that she could lift two men, including Steve. When she just wouldn't chop wood but insisted on lifting people, Steve fled to a piano. In the middle of his tune, there came a *Whack, whack!* Helen had started chopping—though not on camera.

"The title of this song is, of course, 'Chop Sticks,' " Steve announced.

Gina Lollobrigida came to Steve's mike with a chip on her beautiful shoulders. Steve attempted to talk Italian to her and she got offended. Her spokesmen suggested next day that Steve apologize. Steve declined with thanks. Gina later told him thanks for having her on his program.

Steve was probably best when reporting an event that gave him a chance to fool around with his passion for word-twisting.

When the dog-show champions and their trainers came on, Steve said he was more familiar with certain other breeds such as a "hand-woven Afghan," a "wireless telegraph," a "Boston chiropractor," a "double-breasted seersucker," and a "Scotch tippler."

"Steve would rather say or write something funny than do something funny," say his writers. "That makes him one of us."

One man who was being interviewed in the audience told Steve, "My wife's home tonight."

Steve looked into the camera and said, "You've just witnessed a scene from the movie . . . 'Fat Chance.'"

A do-gooder at heart, Steve experimented with reform reporting—showing masked teen-age narcotics addicts and juvenile delinquents. He also attacked racketeers.

"Steve's got more on some of those people than the district attorney," boasted Jayne.

"Our house," she says, "is littered with hundreds of little pieces of paper on which Steve has written ideas for the program or for songs or Broadway shows or books. I carefully collect these and place them on his desk, and they go into a file."

Steve has admirably worked out the problems of child-rearing with his ex-wife, who has since married Andy Young, a musician at M-G-M. The three boys—Brian, Steve, and David—live with their mother in San Fernando Valley but frequently visit their father in New York.

When Steve and Jayne go to California, they sometimes stay at the home of Steve's ex-wife and her new husband.

"The boys are there and it gives Steve more time to be with them," is the explanation. "Besides, it's more convenient for everybody, since there aren't any hotels in the neighborhood."

The name of Bristad Enterprises, Steve's major corporation, is a sort of combination of the first few letters of the sons' names. A music company he's just formed, the Rosemeadow Publishing Corporation, picked up the "Rose" from his mother's name, Montrose, and "Meadow" from Jayne Meadows.

If you ever see Steve helling around a night club falling-down drunk, look again and see if it isn't an impersonator. Aside from his sponsor's beer, which he drank on his program, Steve takes only an occasional port. He doesn't dig night clubs.

"Steve wastes no time in life," his wife says. His hobby is more work. He still writes poems and songs.

He has recently added a new facet: the ability to laugh at himself. When he's tired, he looks more gaunt than usual, and his long neck appears more elongated. One recent night when his own face and throat slid suddenly onto the large screen in the studio, Steve saluted the audience, "Welcome to the Adam's apple hour!"

His mother, who lives now in Los Angeles, has said that Steve "is not a bit nor a whit" sentimental. Still, when he became a father, he promptly wrote a touching poem about it, starting, "I met my son today." Perhaps his mother is fond of word-manipulation, too. Maybe that's where he got it.

We could take one example. When Steve introduced Jayne Meadows to his mother, Steve was tired from many enterprises. His mother served tea.

"Mother," said Steve, "I could use a spoon."

"You look to me like you could use a hearse," said Mother.

"That's why I never open my mouth," Steve told Jayne laughingly. "My mother's always topped me."

Sometimes Steve's efficiency is a little breath-taking.

After he'd licked Ed Sullivan a couple of times, I phoned him that one of my papers wanted me to interview him on the subject: "Isn't Steve doing too much? Isn't he spreading himself thin?"

We made an appointment for an hour and a half later.

When I arrived, Steve greeted me in a robe—and handed me several typed sheets.

"I tried to figure out what questions you'd ask me—and here are the answers," he said.

He'd anticipated practically every question. The interview was disposed of within ten minutes. He felt, of course, that he *wasn't* doing too much, that today an entertainer must entertain—dance, sing, tell jokes. And about the dancing that Steve does: he invented a "dance-o-prompter."

Maybe he couldn't dance, but others could. So he assigned a girl choreographer to go through the dance steps off camera . . . and he simply imitated her steps.

Nobody can accurately foretell what'll happen to this remarkably gifted young man, but in Chicago they're fond of telling how Steve went to meet a local savant who said, "Steve's very promising."

"I didn't promise him a thing!" replied Steve, when he heard about it. Steve's friends contend that with television comedy being the informal commodity it is, Steve, in that remark, promised himself a fortune.

BOB HOPE'S

VITAL STATISTICS:

Born Leslie Townes Hope on May 29, 1903, fifth of six children, at Eltham, England. Moved to Cleveland when four years old. Parents, William Henry and Agnes Townes. Educated at Fairmont Grammar School and Fairmont High School, Cleveland. Married Dolores Reade, the singer, in 1933. Religion, Protestant. Height, five feet eleven; weight, 180 pounds. Home address, 10346 Moorpark Street, North Hollywood, California. Hobbies, golf, writing short stories and comedy sketches. Children, Linda Roberta Theresa, born 1939; Anthony (Tony) Reade, born 1940; Honora (Nora) Avis Mary, born 1946; William Kelly (called Kelly by parents), born 1946. Favorite drink, Scotch.

"OLD DROOP-SNOOT"

Bob Hope always comes through in a pinch . . . or with a pinch.

Bob's one of the few comedians who can pinch a girl verbally. Old Ski-Nose has sex appeal. There's something about his confident swagger that says, "Here I am, girls!"

He's got a lot of oomph for a guy who's been hanging around this planet since May 29, 1903—also a lot of energy, ambition, and money . . . and, I must add, a lot of talent. Because nobody ever takes offense at his gags, be they about a sweater girl whom he tells, "Mustn't point," or Dwight D. Eisenhower, with whom he plays golf. Ike himself applauded Bob's cracks about his golf at some Washington dinners,

particularly Bob's tale that the Eisenhower caddy kept looking at his wrist one day until Ike finally said, "Why do you keep looking at your watch?" Bob maintained that the caddy retorted, "This isn't a watch—it's a compass."

A comedian's severest test comes when all the "prepared ad libs" are useless because the situation suddenly changes.

I saw Bob handle such a predicament masterfully one night.

Although born in Eltham, England, Bob became a Clevelander in 1907 at the age of four, and has always been a loyal Ohioan. ("I went to a very exclusive school in Ohio—a judge had to send you," he has said.) So when the Ohio State football team goes to the Rose Bowl, which is not infrequently, Bob's always called upon to be M.C. at the Big Ten dinner for the Buckeyes.

The crisis came at the 1954 dinner because somebody decided each of the Big Ten schools should be represented there by a beautiful girl.

Then the facts about each girl were written on cards which were given to Bob—but nobody thought to tell Bob that the girls really weren't from those schools at all.

Assuming that each girl was a co-ed from the school she represented, Bob undertook to extract a little local color from them.

He began to get the idea when he asked the girl representing Purdue, "How long have you represented Purdue?"

"About an hour," she admitted.

Bob choked, and went on to the Indiana representative.

"Where are you from?" Bob asked her.

"Los Angeles," she said.

"Los Angeles, Indiana?" inquired Bob.

By now Bob was having more fun and getting more laughs than he could have if the girls had been legitimate representatives. A beautiful and shapely gal waggled up and said she represented Iowa.

"Have you ever been in Iowa?" Bob queried her.

"I've just flown over it," she answered.

"That's the best way to be there," Bob said. "I don't mean

138

to knock Iowa. It's a wonderful place—in fact, Iowa is the garden spot of that particular state."

Looking at his handful of cards, he groaned, "I wonder who wrote these—Lawrence Tierney?"

Hope, William Holden, Jerry Colonna, Gloria de Haven, and Anita Ekberg, the cheesecake queen, were taking off that very night for Greenland to entertain the troops. While I was standing around backstage, Holden began telling me about Hope's fantastic energy. He said Bob and he had been working on their rehearsals at 2 A.M. the night before—but at 8 A.M. Hope was already up, "seeing about the cameras."

"That Hope—I never saw anybody like him," exclaimed Holden.

But just at this moment, Hope was introducing Anita Ekberg to the Big Ten dinner crowd. I wondered just what he could say, of a collegiate nature, about this Scandinavian beauty of the generous bosom, whose entire schooling had been abroad.

"Miss Ekberg," said Bob, "is here representing the University of Southern California."

Looking her over from top to bottom—and she has a lot of top and a lot of bottom—Bob gasped:

"What a campus!"

My first recollection of Bob Hope is of him as a singer.

It was almost twenty years ago, when Bob was just working up to what he calls his "failure" period.

For Bob is convinced that he was a failure for years, and can almost make you believe it.

Anyway, it was 1936, and the name Bob Hope meant very little to me, and not a lot to most other people. He'd been in vaudeville, and in the show "Roberta." And now I was looking at one of the first Broadway shows I'd ever seen, and there was a fellow in it who kept obstructing my view of Jimmy Durante and Ethel Merman.

That was Hope, and the show was "Red, Hot and Blue."

It's strange about memory. Durante and Merman were, to this then uninitiated theater-goer, the Big Names. I've found, in checking since, that Bob had equal billing with them and that he got $1,000 a week.

Furthermore, he sang two songs . . . and he and Miss Merman made one Cole Porter tune famous. It was "Delovely."

Bob'd laid an egg or two on radio by this time, and this show meant a lot. He tried hard . . . sometimes, maybe too hard.

In the show, a girl got branded on her derrière when she sat down on a hot waffle iron.

That girl was, of course, Ethel Merman. Bob clowned considerably when he sang with Ethel, and the stage manager used to write him notes every few days asking him to quit spoiling the songs with his comedy.

He'd desist but only briefly, because he was hell-bent to be a comedian.

Besides, he had a kind of brassy belief in his own judgment, which has sometimes proved 100 per cent right since.

In the previous show, "Roberta," he'd been convinced that he could get a big yok by saying, "Love is like hash. You have to have confidence in it to enjoy it." But the author of the show, Otto Harbach, hadn't been willing to approve. One night he got the permission of Jerome Kern to use it— and it got a big howl. Harbach told him to continue using it, adding that he'd been wrong about it.

"Red, Hot and Blue" gave the scouts plenty of chance to look over Bob and they liked him.

He and Durante had a specialty in which they dressed like hunters and went bang, bang, bang, with their shotguns.

Down crashed the ducks they'd slaughtered with their unfailing aim.

They rested for a moment discussing how unerring they were. Down crashed some more ducks they hadn't even shot at!

Then they'd lean out over the footlights and orchestra pit in another scene—as though about to crash on their heads.

It sounds like Olsen and Johnson, and they've doubtless done it. It's made possible with the help of a special cleat in your shoe, through which a screw in the stage fits, and holds you onto the boards so you can lean as far as you wish.

One night in Boston, Durante yokked it up more than the

script called for. He actually did crash down into the orchestra, breaking a few instruments—but getting laughs.

Out of this show, in which Bob was good but far from a sensation—for, to repeat, I recall him mostly as an obstruction to the view—came a $60,000-a-year movie deal with Paramount, which later made him rich, and a new deal to go on the air, which led eventually to TV, and even greater riches.

"Droop-Snoot" Hope (born Leslie Townes Hope, one of a brood of six) has often declared that he became an amateur boxer as a boy to keep in shape.

"I kept in shape but my nose didn't," he says.

He enjoys claiming he was the best boy in the reform school, which wasn't true. He wasn't in the reform school, but even if he had been, he wouldn't have been the best boy in it. However, he might have been the most ambitious and most enterprising.

He and another kid, Whitey Jannings, used to have a little racket by which they'd win as much as $75 a day copping prizes for footraces at picnics.

"Did we fix the races?" Hope said to me once. "Not exactly.

"I was a very fast runner as a kid . . . which was a big help to me later in vaudeville.

"Picnics were always at Euclid Beach Park or Luna Park, which were forty minutes apart by streetcar. Often the grocers and butchers had their picnics the same time and their races the same hour, which meant we couldn't win both places and would only get half the loot.

"We'd call up and say, 'This is the *Plain Dealer*. We want to take pictures of your races, what time are they?' If they were the wrong time for us, we said so, and they changed them.

"At the picnic, we'd get hold of the starter. He was usually a guy full of gin and a big cigar. We'd ask how he started the races and he'd tell us. We'd get his rhythm down.

"We found out you could get a little head start at picnics because the starters were always so high they never called you back. We would dig holes for our toes. If the opposition looked tough, one of us would bump him right off, and the other would bump him later on. By the time the starter said 'Go' we were twenty feet down the track and nobody ever had much of a chance with us, due to our 'system.'

"One of us would win the 100-yard dash and the other the three-legged race. We might win $35 or $50 at one picnic. Maybe it would only be a sweater.

"We did worth-while things with the money, too. Bought a blowtorch, blackjack, or something, and went on to finer achievements."

Bob quit East High his second year. He was making $8 to $10 a show doing an act. He sang, tap-danced, played the sax, and did blackface.

It was in Greencastle, Ind., where a theater manager asked him to announce the next week's bill, that Bob got his start.

He kidded it—in Scottish dialect, which he'd been practicing for months. They laughed at him, he kept talking. He hasn't stopped since.

"I'd found myself," he says. "Maybe I didn't like what I found, but there I was."

After working smaller cities to develop his delivery, he thought he was ready for Chicago. The agents didn't think so.

"I was more than $4,000 in debt and had holes in the soles of my shoes. A friend managed to get me a one-day engagement in a neighborhood theater. My months of work paid off . . .

"The manager offered me a three-day engagement at a better house.

"It paid off again when the three-day engagement stretched into six months.

"Then to New York . . . a long-term vaudeville contract . . . a screen test . . . which I flunked, so back into vaudeville . . . a job in a Broadway show, 'Ballyhoo,' where I didn't make much impression . . . so back into vaudeville again . . . then some radio . . . and back into vaudeville *again!*"

Bob had about decided now after this successful fling at vaudeville that he was destined for another failure—in radio, screen-testing, etc.

"I hadn't been good on radio and I made up my mind I was going to be," he told me once.

"I figured out that what you had to have to be good was laughs. And if one man couldn't write enough laughs for you, why not get two men? If two could only write one-third as many as you really needed, why not get six?"

The idea was a little revolutionary at the time. Bob took a lot of kidding about all his writers. But as he tells it, he'd been hard up and didn't want that any more. "Why, I'd forgotten whether you eat steak with a knife or drank it out of a spoon," he says.

Hollywood summoned him and other radio performers for a picture, "The Big Broadcast of 1938"—and used him primarily as a singer, for evidently he hadn't quite convinced them yet he was a comic.

His wife, the former Dolores Reade, a pop singer whom he'd married in 1933, wasn't too happy about the song they gave him to do in the first movie.

"I like it," Bob said.

"I don't," she said. Maybe she was thinking how he might try to turn it into comedy, as he had with Ethel Merman.

Anyway, the song, which he sang with Shirley Ross, was "Thanks for the Memory," and it kept him in the movies. It also kept him and the family in money.

In the last decade, I've frequently heard Hollywoodians speak of Bob Hope as "the king," or "the champ," or "the greatest."

So far as I know his official title is still something about "Old Ski-Snoot," but when the stars are drinking and let their toupees down, they express genuine and unrestrained admiration for Bob.

Primarily, they love his willingness to do anything worthwhile. The late Fred Allen said that, "All the helping hands nowadays have moss grown over them from lack of use," but he wasn't thinking of Hope. He won't remember it—but I will: some years ago when I was doing a little radio program from the Belmont-Plaza Hotel, hoping I would have at least one important person there for the opening, I looked up and saw Bob—with Jane Russell yet!

Bob and Jane were playing at the Paramount Theater then and breaking all records . . . *busting* all records, to be exact.

"Bob Hope and Jane Russell—WHAT A TRIO!" exclaimed one columnist, who shall be nameless, since it was me.

One summer the Beautiful Wife and I wished to see the Great Northwest. We wished to get away from those Broadway and Hollywood characters, with whom we were constantly afflicted.

Gradually we arrived in the Badlands of the Dakotas.

We approached Mount Rushmore near Rapid City.

Perhaps you don't know that you can look out of your hotel window in Rapid City and see dinosaurs. They seem quite realistic—to all people accustomed to the sight of dinosaurs—and I'm told that folks wrestling with a hangover are considerably moved when they try to focus their bloodshot eyes on the scenery some morning . . . and come face to face with a dinosaur.

The W.P.A. (Works Progress Administration to you youngsters) built these dinosaurs during the Depression, as sort of a tribute to the dinosaurs that once inhabited these parts.

In the evening you can look out your hotel window and see Indians dancing a war dance across the street in front of a gift shop.

One evening we looked out—and saw Bob Hope.

We weren't surprised. He was appearing that night at the stadium in an open-air show. He was on the way somewhere—London, I think—and was "breaking the jump" by stopping off here to do a show for a fee that would help pay his traveling expenses.

Then there was Oct. 20, 1953, when he was the star of the Ohio Sesquicentennial, and its TV show, emanating from Cleveland.

Bob'd taken his TV program on the road, back to Cleveland, where he'd once been a shoe salesman. Bob wasn't the greatest thing in TV yet, and it took some courage to do a show away from New York or Hollywood. But, if you'll remember, he'd had great success producing his radio shows from outlying army camps during the war, and he still liked the formula.

What a night that was!

About fifty "distinguished Ohioans" had shown up because they'd been promised they were going to be on Bob Hope's TV program before an estimated 25,000,000 viewers.

I knew their attitude, because I was one of them. We had a rehearsal in the afternoon, when we learned that all we would have to do was to sit down and then, possibly, stand up and take a bow when our name was called. Most of us weren't actors, and that was all we cared about doing . . . but we did want to do that . . . inasmuch as our relatives back home would be looking in.

And what a flock of Buckeyes we had!

I can't remember them all, but I know there was Norman Thomas, Louis Bromfield, old Cy Young, Milton Caniff, Charles F. Kettering, Blanche Thebom, Editor Charles Merz of the New York *Times*, the Rev. Norman Vincent Peale, and so on, and so on. . . .

I got a front-row seat in that galaxy for the simple reason that I was physically one of the shortest people in the group.

Many, many things went wrong that night—starting with the lighting and ending with the timing.

We "distinguished Ohioans" weren't truthfully interested in any part of the program but the last couple of minutes when we were to be introduced.

So when Gloria De Haven's song seemed to be eating into the time intended for our very important introductions and bows, we naturally began to hate her. Many of us have hated her ever since, because the majority of those distinguished Ohioans were never seen that night on TV.

Lucky me! Only the first row got introduced!

"I feel very bad about this," Bob told me that night at a little after-show reception at the Hotel Carter. "If I'd had one minute . . ."

And there was reason, for some of the distinguished Ohioans were muttering unkind remarks in their shirtfronts about what their kinfolk back home were going to say. . . .

145

"Yeah, yeah, you're supposed to be a big shot back in Ohio, and they don't even let you on television . . . yeah, yeah!"

That's the way they pictured it, and probably it did happen when they got home. Some of the experts were so hasty as to say that this would be the end of Bob Hope on TV. Bob himself was extremely concerned that night when he got on the phone and called New York and Hollywood for reports on the show. It seems curious now that his TV show has gone onward and upward since, and that one must be a very, very loyal Ohioan, as I am, even to remember the program that seemed then to be such a catastrophe for Bob. . . . "Bob's biggest boo-boo," as one critic called it.

"You keep trying," Bob says. "You get a little better."

That's the way it's always been with Bob and his jokes. He's a master of the monologue, the greatest deliverer of the one-liner.

"I'm glad to be back here to see all the familiar faces," he said in Cleveland, "and all the faces I tried to be familiar with. . . .

"I just came back from England—went over there to case the place and see whether Bing should make them another loan.

"He pays so much taxes now that when the Bomb goes off, it doesn't say 'Bang,' it says 'Bing!' . . .

"But honestly, that movie '20,000 Leagues Under the Sea' was filmed in Bing's swimming pool."

Let Bob receive *Photoplay*'s Award for 1955 and he gushes, "I haven't had such a thrill since Liberace let me feel his shirred-beaver coat."

"The richest man in the country isn't Howard Hughes," Bob says, "but Liberace's dentist."

Bob tells several stars he just saw their last movie, "Blood Alley."

"That's the picture," he explains to his audience, "about the Hollywood Freeway."

The atomic blasts in the Nevada desert are food for Bob's comment. "They did very little damage," he says. "The only difference is that now the gophers are wearing upswept hairdos."

The H-bombs, he understands, will come in three sizes: "The Super Bomb, the Super-Duper Bomb, and 'One of Our Planets Is Missing.'"

He can talk for a week, and may even do so, about such an event as the opening of the new Beverly Hilton Hotel. "It's so swanky," he maintains, "that they won't serve navel oranges unless they're wearing a cummerbund."

When he was hoping to take his TV troupe to Russia, he said, "We were going to do our first show in Moscow, but there's always the possibility of being held over."

Bob deals in topical spoofing, and his gags are almost always funniest when they are the crispest—the moment when they're served. A year or two later they may not be so funny, but they will remind you of Who was Who and Who was News at the time.

Probably more gag writers and comedy creators have lived off Hope than any other comedian. One of the most colorful was little Barney Dean, now dead, whom Hope and Bing Crosby had in partnership until his death.

Little Barney used to ride around the Paramount lot on a bicycle that bore a sign saying, "Barney Dean, Funny Writer."

"I'm a fellow who has a great flair for idleness," Barney used to say as he sat around the set, eyes closed, hat pulled down over his face. According to him, however, he was quite a fashion plate, and his shoes were always shined, and so was his head. Bob once offered to introduce him to a certain beautiful girl.

"Listen," snapped Barney indignantly, "I already got a girl! I don't go in for that sort of thing. What time could this girl be ready?"

Once Barney and Bob got into an argument about who'd pick up the check for dinner for a rather large group . . . a check for about $150. Bob settled it by seizing the check out of Barney's grasp.

"I'll make a deal with you," Barney told him. "You pay for the dinner, and on the way home, I'll pick up the papers."

When Bob began flying practically everywhere entertaining troops and filming TV shows, he had to have Barney with him. Barney got a reputation for being the man who could make Bob laugh.

Barney feared plane rides, however. Once when Bob had managed to get him aboard in the first days of their air trips, the weather was rough, and Barney was sick—and also scared.

Reeling over to Bob, Barney said:

"I'll settle for a concussion right now."

Barney was a writer who seldom wrote anything. Hanging around, watching, Barney might remember, from his vaudeville experience, a gag or a wheeze that could be switched around and inserted into the script. Or, he might get an original idea about "punching up" the routine. Bob always listened respectfully to Barney's suggestions. Besides, Barney was sort of a court jester for Bob. For years, Bob would pick Barney up in his car and drive him to the studio. But . . . Bob never stopped the car.

It was Bob's joke that he would make Barney run and jump on.

Sometimes Barney'd have to run a block.

Barney had befriended Bob away back in 1928, when Bob wasn't Bob yet. Fact is, he'd changed his name from Leslie to Lester, because he thought "Lester" had more sex appeal. As Bob tells the story, he was in Chicago, trying to figure out whether he should return to selling shoes in Cleveland, when he got a job as M.C. at the Stratford Theater.

A dancer in those days, Barney had the respect of Charlie Hogan, the booker, and when Hogan asked him how Hope was doing, Barney said:

"Real good. You'll be hearing about him."

That helped Bob hang on, and his salary went from $175 to $250 a week, then to $300. Bob helped Barney latch on at Paramount years later when he had become big.

Bob's slant on humor is simpler than most comedians' but his consistently high ratings on NBC-TV demonstrate that he's wiser than many others.

He believes in making people laugh at a joke, providing

he thinks it's funny. "You must have the courage to wait," he says.

"Longer than any other comedian has enough guts to wait," he adds. "You have to let them know who's running things."

A comic must draw a line between smart and oversmart material, Bob contends. He used to do a routine with a girl named Louise Troxell, and she'd say that she'd just come back from the doctor. "Well, what about it?" Bob would ask. "Well, the doctor said I'd have to go to the mountains for my kidneys," she'd reply. "That's too bad," Bob would answer. "Yes," she'd say, "I didn't even know they were up there."

One critic has since declared that Bob proved his greatness beyond all doubt—when he got anybody to laugh at such material.

Even today, when he speaks lightly of that sort of thing as his "sophisticated material," Bob doesn't hanker to be thought of as a smart or brittle comic—for he knows they don't get the audiences. However, he can handle smart comedy; his M.C. chores on the Academy Awards from Hollywood have been brilliant. Bob used a line several years ago that clearly established that he has a wondrous sense of humor about himself, his strengths, and his shortcomings. "I have a good bit of trouble about my autographs," he said, taking that long pause that we know so well. "But usually, I can get somebody to take them."

When you look over Bob's last decade, you realize that he's an independent cuss.

Possibly a Texas oil strike had something to do with that. He and Bing came into a considerable chunk of wealth in 1949. They were partners of W. A. Moncrief, Sr. of Fort Worth, in the discovery of a flush production (100 bbl. an hour in this case) in the North Snyder pool in Scurry County in West Texas.

In November, 1954, this property was sold for $21,000,000. Bob and Bing owned 16 per cent each.

I don't know what their investment was originally—but their joint take on the sale was about $7,000,000—and I heard that Bob showed his friend Toots Shor a check for $2,000,000 as part of his share.

So in a little more than a score of years, Bob had worked that $25-a-day act into such a gold mine that he was better-fixed than many of the folks who hired him. He stood up for what he wanted.

A couple of his tiffs were with his NBC bosses because he had Frank Sinatra on his radio show and wished to say, "I will be seeing you tomorrow night, Frankie, on your CBS show."

NBC cut him off the air for a few seconds, just as it had cut Fred Allen off for kidding the NBC vice-presidents.

Paramount suspended Bob once for not agreeing to work on a certain picture. Bob told the reporters, "You have it wrong. I've suspended Paramount."

There was a long difference of opinion with Lever Brothers, which sponsored him on radio. It got to be a personal hassle with Charles Luckman, the "wonder boy" who then headed Lever Brothers.

Bob wished to transcribe many of his radio shows—then a comparative novelty. Luckman disapproved.

Bob had a ten-year contract that would have paid him $10,000,000 had it run the full term. At the end of five years, the differences were so acute that they couldn't continue together.

Lever Brothers announced that it wasn't picking up the option for another year; that Hope was being, in effect, released.

That would have been sensational news, except that Bob had wisely taken all the wind out of it by announcing a couple of weeks earlier that he was asking for his release because the sponsor was giving him "no cooperation."

He had, in effect, fired his sponsor . . . long before Arthur Godfrey had got around to firing.

Luckman subsequently left Lever Brothers for a lucrative architecture business. Hope did all right, too.

Old Droop-Snoot has been pretty inventive about handling his wealth.

He came up with a three-way parlay that would split his

earnings into three corporations. Hope Corporation was to get his book earnings, Hope Records, Inc., would handle his recording loot, and Hope Enterprises would get the receipts from independent movies and personal appearances.

There would have been a profit-and-loss for each corporation and a capital-gains tax only, in case of sale. For a man who was making more than $1,000,000 a year, with a one-sixth interest in the Cleveland Indians baseball team, a piece of the Los Angeles football team, and an interest in a metal company, soft-drink company, and a driving range, it seemed like a good idea. His wealth has increased and increased, until now there's a "Bob and Dolores Hope Charitable Foundation," too.

Today this Bob Hope, still looking terrifyingly young, usually hatless when he swings down the street, unashamed of his slicked-back coiffure that is parted near the middle, needs take no back talk from any of the crewcut comics—for he's getting close to becoming an International institution.

He's been seriously ill just once, in 1951, but he got over the collapse he suffered, in Long Beach, Calif., and can't explain it.

'Way back in 1945 he was reported dead, so this must have been when he really started becoming important. For there's a curious thing that happens in America; let a celebrity get "hot" and the rumor, which can never be traced, spreads with riotlike speed that he's "dropped dead." In this instance, Bob said he wasn't dead; he was merely in Tampa, Fla.

"Are you sure you aren't dead?" I asked, getting him on the phone.

"Wait'll I look in the mirror," he said. He didn't want to be accused of giving false information to the newspapers. Finally he said: "If *I* look dead, you should see Crosby."

It seems incredible now in these days of spectaculars, colossals, etc., that Bob seemed to be sounding a little greedy in 1950 when he asked $50,000 to do his first TV show.

Frigidaire settled for $40,000—Bob making it clear that this was to be just for *his* services.

It was the Easter show, with Dinah Shore, Douglas Fairbanks, Jr., and Bea Lillie helping out. I went up to have a look at the rehearsals at the Nola Studios, upstairs over Lindy's on Broadway. The great composer, Richard Rodgers, was sitting there in this crude, bare room, and I foolishly asked, "Are you on this show, too?"

"No," said Dick. "I'm here to ask him to do a benefit next September." And this man with the magnificent sense of humor, which so many people never find out about due to his genius with melody, said, pretending indignation: "How dare he keep me waiting? Why, I'm here to ask him a favor!"

They did that show from the antiquated New Amsterdam Roof which, if you've never seen, you shouldn't.

On this program, Bob had a line that New Yorkers particularly enjoyed. Vincent Impellitteri—"Impy"—was mayor then, and the papers were always kidding him about his many vacation trips to Florida.

Bob was describing the Easter Parade, with many words about the ladies' elegant finery and the striped pants of the gentlemen.

"Mayor Impellitteri was there," Bob said, "in white tie and suitcase."

Having struggled with great conscientiousness on that program, Bob didn't feel too happy when one reviewer commented, "Comparatively speaking, TV is still a baby, but it doesn't need that much changing."

But old Niblick Nose has gone onward and upward in TV since.

He had to slow up his pace for television; he found out that the machine-gun monologue was too fast, and he had to sell himself as much as or more than his gags. He learned quickly that one can be on the air too frequently. Seeking something different, he went abroad to film his shows.

Always, Ski-Snoot with the slouch pouch made a lot of capital out of the fact that he had a nose that only he could love.

And it always brings back to me a tale that was told me half a decade ago about this same Bob Hope, who eventually became the movies' Number One Box Office Attraction (1949, if you want to look it up. In that year, he passed a star who'd held the title for five years—a gent named Crosby).

I was around backstage at the Coronet Theater, where there was a show called "Tickets, Please!"

Paul and the late Grace Hartman were the stars, and I begged them to tell me an inspirational story.

"Sure," said Paul.

In 1932, a small, intimate revue called "Ballyhoo" caused nothing much but ennui in New York. Bob Hope and the Hartmans were in it—but they were secondary to Willie and Eugene Howard, Gus Shy, Jeanne Aubert, and Lulu McConnell.

"Bob Hope doesn't belong," everybody said.

"He should be fired," everybody agreed.

They tried to get him to quit. He wouldn't. They cut his part to three words, as follows: "Girls, girls, girls!"

The show moved over to Newark, where one star, who was also helping to direct, didn't get his make-up on in time to make the stage   a nasty oversight.

Producer Lee Shubert, happening to be there and witnessing the restlessness in the audience, which seemed about to ask for their money back, inquired passionately, "Who can go out there and do something for a few minutes?"

"I can!" replied the voice of Leslie, later Lester, Hope.

He had some stooges waiting handily, and one of them, Paul Murdock, hollered to him, "Oh, Mr. Hope, your laundry's back!"

Bob paused. Bob waited.

"They refused it," yelled the stooge.

There was a lot more, and Bob stayed in the show, became, in fact, the best thing in it. They discovered him then, and said he was ready to go to Hollywood. That is, some people did. The Hollywood scouts didn't, though.

"That guy," they said, "can never overcome his awful physical handicap."

That's right. His nose.

PERRY COMO'S

VITAL STATISTICS:

Born May 18, 1912, at Canonsburg, Pa., the seventh of thirteen children and the seventh son of a seventh son. Parents, Pietro Como (a mill hand) and Lucia Como, Italian immigrants. Married childhood sweetheart, Roselle Belline, July 31, 1933. Three children: son Ronnie, born January 15, 1940; son David, born April 17, 1946; daughter Terri, born May 2, 1947. Educated Canonsburg High School. Weight, 165 pounds. Height, five feet nine. Brown hair and brown eyes. Eats steaks and chops to keep weight down, avoiding spaghetti. Home, Sands Point, L.I. Hobby, all-weather or any-weather golf, scoring in the 70's. Favorite drink, vodka.

THE BARBER BARITONE

Perry Como started in life as a barber, became a singer, then a millionaire radio and TV star, then a homey kind of a comedian—but several of his best friends today are priests.

One of these priests, young Father Bob Perella, attends Perry's TV rehearsals.

When Perry was doing a run-through of his first program for NBC—just warming up for his titanic battle with his friend Jackie Gleason—Father Perella was watching with friendly interest, along with Julius La Rosa, Frankie Laine, and Rosemary Clooney.

155

Several commercials were rehearsed. Then Perry cleared his throat and announced he was going to sing "Abide with Me."

"Well!" exclaimed the priest. "Even God gets a plug on this show."

After Perry had opened the season singing the Protestant song, he followed this up by singing "*Kol Nidre*," a Jewish chant, on the eve of Yom Kippur.

"Perry, what about our side?" the priest asked Como. And one of Perry's writers told Perry, "Hey, the Mohammedans just phoned and demanded equal time!"

Perry believes in a living religion and enjoyed all that thoroughly. It was a little daring of him to show his religious feelings on his first one-hour show, but as he explained to his associates, "That's the way I feel." Perry is a nonconformist along many lines, and he probably always will be. The idea has worked for him.

For about fifteen years, Perry declined to wear a dinner jacket.

He had an excellent reason. He didn't own one.

Considering that Frank Sinatra's dinner jackets were sheer poetry and that Tony Martin was a fashion-setter with his "After Six" tuxedoes, this was rather shocking to Those Who Care About Such Things. Perry just enjoyed going around in a porkpie hat, tieless sports shirt—and raincoat.

"So when I get an invitation that says 'black tie,'" Perry stated mischievously, at that time, "I make up an excuse not to go.

"I miss more dull parties that way!"

Perry finally bought one for a formal dinner in Washington at which President Eisenhower was to appear. But at the first opportunity he auctioned it off—for charity—for $1500. He was again without a tuxedo and went on missing dull parties.

"The reason for this," Perry said, "is that I had to wear one every night for what seemed like centuries when I was with Ted Weems's band.

"It was always with the stiff front in those days," he groaned, recalling it, "and I swore I would never wear one again if I didn't have to."

156

Then he was given a command invitation to the Alfred E. Smith dinner by Frank Folsom, president of RCA, soon after he went to NBC. As soon as he read the "black tie" part, the old worrying began afresh. He went to see his tailor.

"It looks like I've got to get a dinner jacket, finally," he announced.

"You want me to make you another one?" asked the tailor.

"ANOTHER one?" asked Perry.

"Sure, I've started you five or six dinner jackets."

"No kiddin'!" answered Perry, not remembering.

"Sure, I've got coats for you for one suit, and pants for you for another one, but no pants-with-coat or coat-with-pants that go together."

"What happened? How did you slip up?" Perry asked the tailor.

"*I* didn't slip up!" crowed the tailor. "But *you* would never come in for a fitting!"

The tuxedo-wearing referred to above was one of the reasons that Perry almost gave up singing and went back to barbering around 1941.

He'd just about had it.

"When I left Weems," he says, "I was tired as hell from one-nighters and all that routine, and I figured instead of going out with another band, I might as well return to cuttin' hair. I had my own shop in my home town, Canonsburg, Pa., from the time I was fourteen till I was about twenty-one.

"In my home town the barber was quite a guy. A sage, and adviser, and authority on everything, sort of like the doctor. You lived in the better section of town and were really pretty important.

"So I went home the week before Christmas and laid off for three months, and . . . well . . ."

Hurricane Frankie hit the nation about that time.

Sinatra was panicking the country in the winter of 1942-3 with his crooning at the Paramount Theater and the Rio-bamba, a café that no longer exists.

There were nine crooners crooning their larynxes out in

nine different New York night clubs. Frankie was luring the females into the Riobamba. Every other club was trying to get a good-looking crooner to compete with Frankie. Dick Haymes got his start about that time at the old La Martinique (which also no longer exists).

Agent Tom Rockwell got Como on the phone and painted a picture of the gold that was waiting for every young man who had tonsils with sex appeal.

Como didn't decide instantly. He thought it over.

Whereas Sinatra was driving the dolls daffy in February and March, 1943, Como didn't make his big splash until June 10 of that year.

To make big money on records, he'd have to get known. He agreed to go on a New York sustaining radio show for $76 a week, though he'd been getting $125 with Weems.

"They said that first I should go into a night club and suffer a little," he says.

Perry was well past thirty then . . . considerably older than the other crooners. As Sinatra had made the gals swoon, the press agents suggested that "Como would put them in a coma."

While the new singer was good he didn't cause any hysteria, and wasn't any smashing, sensational hit . . . for I mentioned in my review that "He sang slowly—a little too slow, some people thought."

"He sang mannishly and well," I reported—that was considered important because of the female trade—"and Frank Sinatra and Phil Brito, other top crooners, were there to tell him he was terrific.

"While he didn't make the gals swoon, he got strong applause."

Como did, however, demonstrate a quality that has made him important in television. He started slow—but he grew on you.

He went in for two weeks . . . but stayed sixteen. At the end of four months, he was made. He was booked into the Paramount Theater, he got the call to make records and to go to Hollywood, and was on his way to big money on the radio.

Perry'll ask you to believe that when his agent, Tom Rock-well, proposed that he go into the Copacabana, one of the Copa bosses said:

"Como? Como? Isn't that a lake? What is he, a swimmer?"

Perry'd had his wife, Roselle Belline Como, whom he'd married at twenty-one, along on those one-nighters with Ted Weems . . . and also their child, Ronnie. Perry got exasperated with traveling when they had to heat Ronnie's Pablum on the radiator of the band bus.

"Can I stay put in New York?" Como wanted to know when Rockwell asked him to forget the barbering and come to the Big Town.

"You can stay put," Rockwell promised him.

So Perry was soon on the way to Hollywood.

He found the life there too lush for his tastes. His father'd been a mill hand at the Standard Tin Plate plant in Canonsburg. Only a year or two before, Perry'd seriously considered barbering for $60 to $70 a week. Now when he went to a Hollywood party, a butler leaped up to direct him to the bathroom and practically piloted him to the door.

"I'm not claiming Roselle and I ever give parties half as good," Perry said.

"But I think we do have more fun. The gals stay upstairs and the guys slip down to the cellar and get out the dice or play a little poker and sing like crazy, and next day we remember what we did and we're still speakin', and we call each other up and say, 'Hey, that was okay. Let's do it again.'"

The young Como of those days was thinner-faced, and had more hair . . . he looked something like Julius La Rosa does today. But his loose walk and aversion to ties suggested Bing Crosby.

There were critics who thought he was imitating Bing, although he was probably much more like Russ Columbo, whom he'd known while doing one-nights.

Hollywood didn't know exactly what to do with this sudden juke-box favorite.

"Prisoner of Love," "If I Love You," and "Till the End of Time" were rolling toward the million mark. Twentieth

Century-Fox threw him into "Something for the Boys," and Perry confidently predicted, "This will not only ruin me, but also Hollywood."

They had him do some acting. Something happened to some of that film.

It got lost. It was never seen again.

But enough of it remained to embarrass the devil out of Perry when he took his wife and son to see it at the Roxy in New York when Ronnie was five.

"Why does Daddy keep kissing that woman?" Ronnie kept asking his mother. "Why does he?"

When Como returned to New York to perform at the Versailles and other cafés between pictures, in 1944 and 1945, the Broadway columnists made much of him being the "Vigorous Vocalist," and the noncollapsible crooner. They were all kidding Sinatra about being as muscular as a pipe cleaner, and I mentioned that Como "stood there the way healthy crooners should—without holding onto the mike."

Perry's preference for the simple life comes naturally. His mother, over in Pittsburgh, still doesn't speak much English.

"She thinks anybody making over $75 a week is stealing it—and she's probably right," Perry says.

Perry remembers that when he was getting to be a very big man on the radio and quite proud of his comparative success some years ago, he made one of his frequent trips home. In Pittsburgh his program hadn't been heard for a few days, because of a rearrangement of the station's line-up. Perry was able to explain this to everybody . . . nearly everybody.

"My mother was a little hesitant about asking me," he remembers, "but finally said to me, 'Tell me, did you lose your job?'"

With simple eloquence, Perry has described his father, Pietro, who like his wife, Lucia, was an immigrant, as a "saint who didn't realize it." Pietro at first was a miner, and he begat thirteen children. It sounds like a press agent talking, but Perry was the seventh son of a seventh son.

For several years, Perry and Roselle worried because they

hadn't been married in the church, though they were of the same religion.

"Why didn't we? Oh, I was busy playing one-nighters . . . of course," Perry added quickly, discussing it with me, "that's no excuse."

So his good friend Father Roberts married them here in the church a few years later. Perry hesitates to discuss his religious feelings. To him, it seems like he's bragging about something that shouldn't even be mentioned.

"I have a great deal of respect for priests, and I love to have them around," he says, "because they think a lot better than I do. My boy, you know, is an altar boy."

Unquestionably Perry's one of the most reasonable of all the stars. I saw a couple excellent examples of this trait.

He carries a golf club around almost like Darryl Zanuck totes a polo mallet. One afternoon following the beginning of his 1955-56 season for NBC, I dropped around to the "Show Case" rehearsal hall on Eighth Avenue at Fifty-sixth Street. It was right above an Eighth Avenue landmark known as "The Horse's Tail Saloon."

Accustomed as I am to the strange nooks and crannies that are used for TV rehearsing in New York—I remember once seeing Faye Emerson rehearsing in a Turkish bath—I still doubted if this could be the place.

I was, however, soon in a comfortable-looking outer office, where several actors were waiting and where a nice young man at the desk told me, "Go right in that door there."

There sat Perry, Patti Page wearing glasses, and Peter Lawford huddled beside her, both bent over their scripts.

Perry was reading. I tiptoed over to the side.

A phone rang, and somebody beckoned to Perry. He stopped everything and took the call. Then he walked with his famous easy gait over to where I was sitting. Just then the phone rang again.

"Boy," said one of his staff workers to Perry, "answer the phone!"

Perry smiled. The whole operation had halted, and I felt regretful.

"You haven't time to talk to me," I said.

"We'll make time." Perry picked up the golf club, which had been leaning against the wall, and started swinging it as though he was glad to get away from the grind.

Something had disturbed him about his first show, he confessed.

He had hurt the feelings of a lot of Arthur Godfrey's fans, and he was sorry.

You might recall that on his NBC premiere, Julius La Rosa popped on for a quick bow, and advised Perry to remember one quality he should retain at all times:

"Humility."

It was already a rather old joke, and a few critics didn't care for it. But the loyal Godfrey fans pelted Perry with mail of a very harsh type, and he was overflowing with remorse.

"I've got to do something about it," Perry said, pouring his heart out to me. "I don't know whether to do it on the program or just write Godfrey a letter.

"His fans all tell me something that is quite true. Godfrey has always been very nice to me and said wonderful things about me.

"Then I had to go on and say something about La Rosa 'going on to bigger and better things.' It wasn't very funny. People don't know that when we sit around here and make jokes like that, we don't necessarily mean anything by it, and we didn't in that case. But the point is now I've got to do something about it."

(And he did. He apologized—on the air.

His advisers begged him for half an hour not to do it.

Perry opened his program with his apology regardless of what they'd told him.

That was his way of doing things.)

I also asked Como whether he had felt when he started out in show business that he was primarily a singer or could possibly be a comedian.

He went on swinging the golf club.

Peter Lawford and Patti Page were still waiting.

I was still feeling guilty.

"If I ever hoped to be an out-and-out comedian," he said, "I'd say No.

"But you see, on an hour show, you can't go around singing songs for a whole hour. So we tried to do a few little light things on our first show. And a lot of people said I should stick to my singing!

"It kinda hurts a little," he admitted, "after you've worked a whole week trying to be a little funny . . . and they say you should stick to your singing.

"But," he added, using the line that he practically always uses when somebody criticizes him, "they're probably right."

Perry took another poke at an imaginary golf ball. It was just a putt this time.

Actually, though, the critics may be wrong. For Perry may be slow-moving in one direction sometimes, but he gets there by steady locomotion.

With characteristic leisureliness, Perry had a swimming pool built at his Sands Point home, primarily for Ronnie, a born water rat now taller than his father. Perry talked about the project for about five years and, one day, accomplished it.

Reporters aren't invited to Perry's home, which is full of religious relics and statuary which they might not understand. Roselle is the "kind of a woman who enjoys life when the servant quits."

One day Perry heard that a maid-of-all-work had left and came home expecting to find somebody new installed.

A woman down on her knees scrubbing the floor looked up at him in a curious way as he approached, and he gave her a friendly nod, wondering whether he should introduce himself.

He decided not to and proceeded. The scrubwoman suddenly called out, "So you didn't recognize your own wife!"

Frequently when Perry gets involved in something requiring an important decision he says, "Let me think about this overnight." He brings in the decision next day—which he has reached after talking it over with Roselle.

Probably Como's greatest asset—even greater than his voice—is his likableness.

Well aware of this, and a nice guy first and last, Perry has resisted all attempts to make him a brassy Broadwayite.

When he started doing comedy on his new show, he soon told his staff that he didn't want to do the usual "insult jokes."

The Godfrey incident may have helped convince him— but Perry's instincts were against all insult jokes . . . for him.

When Maurice Chevalier was on his program, the writers wished to refer to the Frenchman as the "Liberace of the Stone Age." Perry nixed that. A line saying Chevalier was quite a man with the girls—"a Chevalier with a hydromatic clutch"—also failed to get his okay.

Then there was a routine about Warner Bros. Theaters all over the world. With Christine in mind, the writers wished to refer to the Copenhagen house as the "Warner Sisters' Theater."

Soft-spoken, clean-living, home-loving Perry didn't feel that this joke fitted his character, either.

He didn't want to be a stand-up Broadway comedian anyway.

Perry had a series of conferences with Goodman Ace and the other writers and outlined his own conception of himself, throwing in some ideas about comedy. Goodman Ace admitted they were good, furthermore, very sensible.

Perry suggested that he be kept the homey type.

He'd done an interview with Rosemary Clooney which had been mostly about records and the music business. Perry felt it could have been made more believable if he'd asked Miss Clooney for an autograph for his boy.

He went on and sketched in the dialogue.

"Oh, certainly," Rosemary would have said. "I just love little boys."

Perry: You'll do it then?

Rosemary: Certainly! How old is your little boy?

Perry: Oh, he's sixteen.

Goodman Ace feels that Como would have to make a million bad jokes before his public would get angry at him.

"He's a little like Eisenhower," says Ace. "When the President makes a mistake, the public says, 'Oh, that must have been Dulles' fault,' and when Perry does anything wrong, they say, 'Oh, that wasn't Perry. That was his writers.' "

Still, Perry knows that there's a big audience out there,

and that it isn't all the homey type. On one show, Ace gave Perry a scholarly line, *"C'est la* TV."

While it didn't exactly delight Como, he accepted Ace's advice, and delivered it perfectly. Some of the culture-vulture TV critics commented favorably on it . . . *they* understood it.

But Perry doesn't like oversmart comedy.

On the third show, Ace wished to have Frank Gallup, the announcer, say, "The jokes are not canned, the music is not canned, and even after two weeks, our star has not been." Perry also asked them to drop that one.

Perry's one major extravagance is his attentiveness to friends.

Sometimes this takes the form of telegrams.

After he's watched a TV performance by somebody he likes, Perry may send off a 500-word congratulatory wire, or he may telephone and give constructive suggestions. Curiously, he and Jackie Gleason are friends, though pitted against each other by the strange fate of network competition. When Gleason had a home near his, Jackie heard something amazing and wonderful, from his viewpoint—Perry had a pool table.

You might have to go miles in that neighborhood to find anybody suddenly interested enough in the better things of life to have a pool table. Jackie demanded the right to beat his neighbor at the game, which he had mastered long ago. In fact, Jackie often claims he is an "old pool hustler."

First, though, Jackie had to penetrate Perry's kitchen.

It sounds easy. But Perry's mother-in-law is an incurable kitchen-sitter. Give her any part of the lush $100,000 home, and she sniffs at it contemptuously. She likes to sit in the kitchen.

Besides, she's a Gleason fan.

"Hel-l-LO MO-MMMMMM!" Jackie would howl as he raised his hand and did the famous Gleason slide into the kitchen. There was no leaving. He had to sit down and talk over things with Mrs. Belline. Both enjoyed it thoroughly . . . even if it did postpone the pool game somewhat . . . and all the time Gleason had such an itch to play.

At last the old pool hustler tangled with the onetime barber across the green-cloth table.

Perry won.

Another Como pleasure is eating.

After a program's just history, he sometimes takes Roselle to Max Asnas' Stage Delicatessen, at Fifty-fourth Street and Seventh Avenue, where Max, "the pastrami pundit," "the corned-beef Confucius," helps load them up with sandwiches, pickles, blintzes, sour cream—everything needed for a picnic . . . at home.

The Comos know they'd have no rest trying to eat at one of Max's tables, for the Broadway mob would be on top of Perry very fast.

Although a member of the Sands Point Country Club, along with such swells as Herbert Bayard Swope, Howard Dietz, and others, Perry usually golfs simply on the Garden City links.

Sometimes he's with his close friend, Peter Lind Hayes. Sometimes he joins music-man Tuti Camaratta. Or he may be swinging against a song-plugging friend who would find the Sands Point Country Club air too rich. Perry also has no compulsion about buying a new car every year. He drove a Cadillac for five years, and only recently felt he'd better get a new one. For Roselle . . . well, that's different . . . he got her a Thunderbird.

A lot of the credit for the smoothness of the Como operation should go to Perry's brother-in-law, Dee Belline, a small, peppery, mustached little man who's always there. He sees to it that everything Perry wants, Perry gets.

With one exception.

He plays golf with Perry.

And Perry loses.

Phil Harris has been striving to get Perry to spend more time in California—because of the year-round golf.

Como has actually discussed buying a house there. His early lukewarmness toward the Hollywood life seems to have changed somewhat. He might get a home there just to use a month or two a year. But if he were there, he would soon be doing movies again—"and I want to take it a little easy," he says. "I don't want to finish a television season one day and start a movie the next. A man with a family . . ."

Sunday is Perry's biggest day of the week—it's his day off . . . and his only one.

"We get all the characters together that day," Perry says, speaking of his family and a few close friends.

"We go to church, we have a big breakfast, and then sometimes I go out and play a few holes. But the old feeling isn't there when you only play once a week."

Perhaps because he himself came from a large family, Perry considers family life more important than many stars do. You seldom see him "around the traps." He likes the Amalfi restaurant in New York—or any other one where you can get good *paisan* food and meet some fellow singers—but he prefers his Sands Point hearthside to the hot spots.

Of course, son Ronnie is a major interest.

One day Perry was unusually happy around his office. He explained to one friend that Ronnie—who's been attending St. Francis Xavier High on West Sixteenth Street in Manhattan, commuting daily by cab, bus, and subway from Sands Point— had mentioned to his parents that he'd thought of entering the priesthood.

"Roselle and I both think it would be a wonderful thing if Ronnie were to feel the call," Perry said.

But that decision's in the future, as are Ronnie's own crooning potentialities. His voice is changing now, and nobody knows whether he might be another Gary Crosby.

Son David, six years younger than Ronnie, and daughter Terri, seven years younger than Ronnie, go to St. Peter's Parochial at Sands Point.

Perry has two corporations to handle his business . . . both with son Ronnie's name in them. There's Roncom Music Company, at 1270 Sixth Avenue—the "Ron" stands for Ronnie, the "Com" for Como—where Perry carries on all his music business. He has a tape recorder, which he uses to tape little personal messages to disc jockeys. Perry credits the disc jockeys with helping him hit the million mark with his records. He doesn't overlook the distributors, however, and took time during one of his vacations to visit even the smaller ones in remote sections of the country.

On Monday morning, Perry arrives at this office, which is on the twenty-third floor of the Americas Building, at Fiftieth Street and Sixth Avenue, and meets Mitch Ayres, his conductor for TV and for recordings.

He plans his song schedule for the TV program two weeks ahead. The comedy part he lays out only one week ahead. Perry knows that it's his singing that sells Como.

On Tuesday, Perry goes to his other office—Roncom Productions, on Fifth Avenue and Forty-ninth Street. It's referred to there as "the penthouse," but this may be an exaggeration. It does have a narrow terrace. Here, in a conference room where Perry presides without a tie, he meets Lee Cooley, his producer; Goodman Ace, and the others to plot out the non-music part of the program.

Not exactly a quick study, Perry learns his script by plodding through and by "taking it easy."

"I don't use the TelePrompTer on straight dialogue," Perry says, "because I don't like to be looking over people's heads.

"But on songs I have the TelePrompTer going showing me the lyrics—just in case everything turns black some night."

Perry's found the recruiting of guest stars something of a headache. One of his good friends, Rocky Marciano, couldn't go on his show the week he'd licked Archie Moore, for the good reason that somebody who'd been in the guest-star-interviewing field of TV much longer had tied Rocky up to be on his show.

"Rocky wanted to do it for me, but, well . . ." said Perry, telling me about it.

Perry got Archie Moore, however, and everything ended happily because Archie presented him at the end of the program with the skipping rope he'd used in training for the Marciano fight.

"My boy's going to get a kick out of having this for his room," beamed Perry.

All the new problems haven't changed Perry's good humor. He continues to make little jokes with himself as the target.

"My doctor tells me I haven't got ulcers," Perry said one night backstage, "so how come all these pains in my stomach?"

But actually he feels he can take it easy because of his firm deal with NBC, which knows he's going to be one of the greats in the business.

"NBC has given me just twelve years to make good," Perry says sometimes in his warm-up or in little after-the-show talks to the audience.

But always there's the hint in his speech that he's not at all dedicated to show business, like Milton Berle.

Not long ago a young Texas minister who was preaching on radio came to New York to get interviews with various stars who were sincerely interested in religion. Perry Como gave him one of his best interviews. After it was tape-recorded and the zealous young pastor was about to set forth for Texas on his soul-saving mission, Perry asked him, "How'd you like to swap jobs?"

EDDIE FISHER'S

VITAL STATISTICS:

Born Edwin Jack Fisher in Philadelphia, August 10, 1928; one of seven children. Educated Gratz and Southern High, Philadelphia. Sang in synagogue choir at nine, and on WFIL at thirteen. U.S. Army soloist, 1951; discharged April 10, 1953. Gold-plated records, "Any Time," "I'm Walking Behind You," "Oh, Mein Papa," and "I Need You Now." Married Debbie Reynolds September 26, 1955, at Grossinger, N.Y. Daughter, Carrie Frances, born October 21, 1956.

Height, five feet seven; weight, 138. Hair, black. Sports, water-skiing and swimming. Drinks, Coca-Cola.

Hobby, singing.

HE LIVES TO SING

Away back in Eddie Fisher's before-Debbie Reynolds days, I was in London waiting for the Coronation . . . and so was Eddie . . . and so was Princess Margaret.

On the afternoon of May 20, 1953, I dropped in at Eddie's suite in the Savoy Hotel to ask about this and that.

"I have to go to a ball for Princess Margaret tonight—would you like to go along?" asked Eddie.

There was some excitement in his manner, and I quickly accepted.

"It's the Red, White and Blue Ball, and it's at the Dorchester," Eddie informed me happily.

This was in Princess Margaret's before-Peter Townsend

days. Not exactly before, but before the news of her romance with the group captain had been published. It was whispered about, but everybody seemed to realize then that it could never result in a marriage. It seems strange, thinking back to it now, that everybody considered then that nothing would come of it . . . that everybody changed opinions later . . . and still later, changed them once more.

Anyway, there was Eddie Fisher saying to me:

"If you'll meet me at my dressing room, right after the Palladium we can go on over together. Black tie, of course."

You couldn't blame him for being a little excited.

The little boy from Philadelphia who had been discovered by Eddie Cantor on the resort circuits in the Catskills was not only starring at London's greatest theater, the Palladium— but he was receiving messages from a princess.

When we stepped out of our limousine at the Dorchester, we found a red carpet laid out on the sidewalk for Princess Margaret to walk on.

I wouldn't lie to you. We walked on it, too. After all—I'm the Earl of Wilson. We waited in an anteroom until it came Eddie's time to sing, and then I walked out into the big ballroom with him to see him perform before this tough crowd.

Eddie was nervous. But the princess sent word that he shouldn't be. She said, too, that she knew Eddie's records, and that she would lead the applause herself, and hoped he would sing, among others, "Outside of Heaven."

Maybe you don't remember it. It was a very sad love song. The theme was that Heaven was a house in which the adored one resided. The singer was lamenting about his love for the adored one within as he walked along in front of the house . . . "Outside of Heaven."

"Passing your house with misty eyes" was one line.

The princess' request for this song was taken by us to be an indication of her torchiness for Captain Townsend, and inasmuch as the romance was a big secret then, the request became all the more poignant to us.

Eddie sang several songs at the mike, with the princess smiling at him from across the room, and personally leading the gloved hand clapping.

Then Eddie was summoned to her to be presented.

The princess was in a nest of nobility—young lords and princes. There were Prince Nicholas of Yugoslavia, Viscount Hambleton, Lord Blandford, Lord Plunkett, and others. When Eddie approached, Margaret arose at her table and extended her hand. Eddie shook it and addressed her as "Ma'am"—as he'd been advised to do by some London experts on royal matters.

Margaret called him Eddie.

They chatted there for about fifteen minutes. Some of the young lords got nervous about Margaret paying so much mind to a Yankee crooner. I was standing a few feet away from the table, hoping to be presented to the princess, and sure enough, one of the young lords suddenly swung around and beckoned to me.

"Now I'm going to be presented, hooray, hooray!" I thought . . . and I shot right over.

"Waiter, some more champagne!" commanded the young lord.

Finally the princess ended her chat with Eddie. Not, I gathered, that she wished to, but because she had to go out to the center of the ballroom and present some prizes, including a cookstove, which had been drawn in a door-prize raffle.

But before she flew off, the princess asked Eddie to sit down at the main table and ordered that he be introduced around. He promptly got into conversation with titled young men, and even women. Some of the young men wore medals and accents.

When the party broke up, Eddie and his manager, Milton Blackstone, took us to a club for supper—and Eddie was truly entranced.

"Nothing like this has ever happened to me before," he exclaimed. "Princess Margaret's just wonderful. Our conversation just flowed. Maybe this should never have happened. I probably won't be able to sleep. Do you know she has really beautiful eyes! I think after this I'd better get married real soon."

It seemed to me that Eddie, whom so many girls wanted

to marry, realized that he'd suddenly found somebody who was unattainable to him.

Eddie flew back to New York and never met Margaret again.

A few months later I saw Eddie with Debbie, and mentioned to him jokingly the big page-one story about Margaret and Captain Townsend.

Eddie took Debbie by the arm.

"I've got my own princess now," he said.

Eddie's friends are always delighted to recall how an expert on Broadway show business persuaded him, briefly, to change his name when he was just starting his career.

"You can never get anyplace with a name like Eddie Fisher," the man told him.

And Eddie believed him, and obeyed.

Actually, of course, Eddie's story is precisely the pattern of the Horatio Alger, Jr., stories of a generation ago—Eddie in real life was probably poorer than some of the Alger heroes and now he's richer than the Alger heroes got to be. Eddie doesn't mind confessing that as a kid he helped his father, Joseph Fisher, peddle vegetables in South Philadelphia. Eddie's earliest public singing was in the role of a street peddler singing out such words as "Tomatoes, nice ripe tomatoes, nice fresh corn!" If you want to be romantic about that, you can say Eddie was a street singer.

The family was briefly on relief in those Depression days.

Eddie was one of seven children—near the middle—and he remembers going to the railway station where flour and vegetables were handed out to relief families. He was ashamed of being a relief recipient and used to hide the food under his coat.

The shirts given out to relief families were usually striped and Eddie didn't like wearing them.

"Everybody'll know," he thought.

But, just as in the Alger stories, wealth and fame awaited him. There's quite a little chunk of folklore already built up about Eddie. One version alleges that when he was born (Edwin Jack Fisher), on August 10, 1928, the nurses of

Philadelphia Northern Liberty Hospital sang him to sleep to the tune of "Climb upon My Knee Sonny Boy"—from the then current Al Jolson movie.

Looking back on it now, practically everybody remembers prophecies about his singing. His grandmother is said to have forecast that "this one will be something special."

At nine, Eddie was already singing as an assistant to the cantor of a synagogue. He'd won some singing prizes at five and six, and his mother had asked a music professor to hear him.

"In his throat there is a thread of gold," the professor purportedly remarked.

The professor wasn't speaking of money, but that's how it turned out.

When Eddie was about thirteen, he arrived one day at Station WFIL, in Philadelphia, with a little blond girl about his age, who told the producers of a children's show that she'd brought them two great singers; herself and Eddie.

His voice was untrained and rough, but he had such power in it when he let go that he was promptly hired—for fifteen cents a day in trolley-car tokens.

Eddie was extremely bashful and ill at ease in those days. He was cast as the hero in a radio serial called "The Magic Lady," and at the end of each show, he'd be in some crisis so full of suspense that you were supposed to listen to the next one to see how he got out of it.

At fifteen, Eddie hadn't yet become convinced that he had any particular aptitude because he said in answer to a questionnaire at Gratz High that he would like to be "either a pharmacist or a musician" when he grew up.

By the time he was seventeen Eddie was out of school—without a diploma, which he later earned in the Army. He had another piece of paper, though; a contract.

It was a contract stating that Skipper Dawes, a Philadelphian who'd engaged him originally on the children's show, should manage him. Eddie sang for several bands, for Buddy Morrow and for Charlie Ventura, among others. But he hadn't hit his stride yet, and Dawes, realizing he couldn't handle him very well from Philadelphia—for Eddie was "trying it in New York" by now—tore up the contract.

Like many a singer before him, Eddie got an audition at the Copacabana.

Times were tough for him then. He and a friend had a very small two-room apartment on Fifty-second Street. He often didn't have rent or food money. The band singing jobs didn't last, and they didn't pay much, anyway. Frequently Eddie was ready to give it all up.

The Copacabana was then managed by Monte Proser, who has discovered much great talent.

Eddie auditioned, he has since said, "in a dim room where a lot of charwomen were cleaning up."

Proser is a night owl who believes that everything worthwhile happens after sundown and before sunrise. To him, the ideal time for a business conference is about 3 or 4 A.M. — "By this time," according to him, "everybody's had their coffee and is fully awake."

For Proser, Eddie only had to sing one chorus.

For Eddie could belt a song forcefully enough for it to be heard above the orchestra. Proser, of course, didn't have Eddie in mind as starring at the Copacabana yet, but to sing the "production numbers"—as most singers don't have the strength to be heard.

"When you're old enough," Proser told him because Eddie hadn't yet reached eighteen, "you've got a job here at $100 a week."

That, anyway, is the way the story is generally told. But it's recounted somewhat differently by Proser.

"I'll tell you exactly how the guy started with me," Proser told me not long ago. "I had a guy working in the Copa with me named Manny Mangle. He's still there and I'm not.

"He had a brother named Ira Mangle, who knew a boy named Eddie Fisher.

"Eddie was about seventeen then. I used to audition acts every Tuesday. Manny Mangle wanted me to listen to Eddie Fisher because he was a friend of his brother, Ira Mangle.

"So I told Manny Mangle to tell Ira Mangle to tell Eddie Fisher to come to the audition.

"So this Tuesday Eddie Fisher came in and sang a little, and I said, 'Stop right there.' I said to him, 'Wait over there.'

"I guess he thought he was through right away. Because afterward when I talked to him he said, 'Ira Mangle told me to come see you.'

"I said, 'Yeh, yeh, I know. But you're too young yet to work at the Copa. But when you're eighteen, come in and you can sing the production numbers.'"

Proser thinks the salary promised Eddie was $60 a week, but the legend is that it was $100 a week and that's what Eddie seems to remember. He probably would know better than Proser; after all, it meant more to him.

As for Eddie's reaction to Proser's announcement that he had a job as soon as he was eighteen:

Proser recalls that Eddie said, "Oh, my gosh!" and Proser didn't know whether Eddie was protesting that it wasn't enough money, or exulting that it was too much.

Actually, Eddie was expressing surprise that he'd passed the Copa's test and been promised a job there at probably the best-known café in the world. And—he had almost passed out at the money.

That summer, after he'd been promised the Copacabana job, he got well acquainted with a man named Milton Blackstone, later to become his manager, and who was with him in London at Coronation time.

So many stars have "worked the mountains" and found them a great training ground, that Proser suggested this course for Eddie.

And who could arrange it more expertly than Proser's friend and ofttimes business associate, Milton Blackstone, advertising man, industrialist, and publicist for the world-famous resort hotel Grossinger's.

Off to the Catskills went Eddie—and it's remembered there that he was well-liked, although far from sensational just yet.

I'm sorry to confess that Eddie didn't strike me as phenomenal when he opened at the Copa that autumn. But then few production singers do knock the customers dead. They're just part of the show's preliminary build-up toward the appearance of the big star you've come there to see. Many

177

customers would be happier if all the production folderol were eliminated. Sometimes the customers go so far as to say, "There's a boy who could go someplace if he got the right breaks—I wonder what his name is?"

They may even look at the program to see who he is—but after they've found out they usually forget it.

Eddie was discouraged again after the Copa job didn't make him famous.

He had decided by now that nobody goes to the Copacabana to hear a singer—unless the singer is a Lena Horne or a Joe E. Lewis, or Frank Sinatra.

And since he was none of these, he accepted out-of-town jobs arranged for him by Val Irving, who preceded Blackstone as his manager. Blackstone didn't come into the picture as his actual manager until much later.

When Eddie returned to New York after that touring, he was booked into a little downstairs spot on Broadway known then as the Riocabana.

He heard once more the complaint, "You'll never get anywhere with a name like Eddie Fisher"—and agreed to change it to something considered much, much more distinctive; Dick White.

Dick White! Is it any more glamorous, any more exciting, than Eddie Fisher? It seems ridiculous now, but shows how hard Eddie was trying, and how much he was listening to anybody who had a suggestion for improving him or his chances of "making it."

The Riocabana was a comedown for Eddie after the Copacabana.

"The Copa's a showcase," agents always say.

The biggest stars appear there. The biggest names come in. You have a chance to be seen by somebody who might do something for you.

Hardly any names came into the Riocabana. Hardly any no-names came in. Hardly anybody, in fact, came in. So Dick White didn't advance himself any further than Eddie Fisher had.

Frequently Dick White borrowed money to get along.

When the summer came, he worked some more in the

mountains, and still nobody thought he was the greatest thing since Sinatra—except maybe his mother in Philadelphia.

"He got very discouraged," recalls Monte Proser.

"He got on a bus and went back to Philadelphia.

"He told his mother he'd had it. He was nineteen, and he was going to give up."

After a long talk with her, though, he decided to call up Milton Blackstone. "Come up to Grossinger's this weekend," Blackstone said.

Cynical people who don't believe that Horatio Alger stories happen in real life will argue with me about what came next. It was many weekends later, at Grossinger's—a summer later, in fact—that it happened. But it did happen.

Eddie Fisher, then twenty years old, belted out a few songs one Sunday . . . whereupon Eddie Cantor bounced out of his seat and onto the bandstand with his saucer-eyes flashing.

He must have been doing his "If You Knew Susie Like I Know Susie" strut as he said, "Ladeeeez and gennnnnl-mun . . ."

And there was silence at Grossinger's—one of the few times.

"I've heard many a crooner in my day"—the eyes rolled—"but this boy isn't a crooner. HE'S A SINGER! AN ARTIST! I want this boy to go with me on my cross-country tour. Okay, Eddie?"

"YOU BET, MR. CANTOR!" gasped Eddie Fisher.

From then on Eddie Fisher was in—although there were detours, roadblocks.

Cantor taught the younger Eddie a lot on that tour. He gave him an overcoat and a gold wristwatch, and allowed him to drive his car to California. Eddie wasn't making a lot of money . . . wouldn't be for a long time . . . but Blackstone believed in the boy's future.

Just being known as Cantor's discovery meant much to Fisher.

People thought of him . . . people who'd never thought of him before. Back in 1950 there was a swank spot just across the George Washington Bridge, in New Jersey, known as Bill Miller's Riviera. A new highway project has since caused its demolition. But the Riviera—known in earlier years as Ben

Marden's Riviera and famous as a plush gambling spot prior to World War II—was then an expensive summer-night rendezvous, which also opened for New Year's Eve.

All the greats starred there . . . Sophie Tucker, Harry Richman, Joe E. Lewis.

Singer Fran Warren was scheduled to star there on New Year's Eve 1950—with Danny Thomas—but she was taken ill.

Bill Miller looked around . . . and decided to take a chance on Eddie Fisher.

Eddie was frightened about it. Who was he to go into a spot where only the big stars had worked? His manager urged him on. Eddie Fisher was a sensation that New Year's Eve, which is pretty remarkable in itself, since experience with New Year's Eves has been that hardly anybody ever remembers what happened. The newspapers take some pictures of the revelers—usually the afternoon before—and little else ever gets into the record.

However, that was the beginning of the Big Time for Eddie. All the Copacabana and Riocabana stuff up to that time was bush league by comparison.

RCA Victor had taken him on a few months before, and in 1950 "Thinking of You"—his fourth record for the label—made up for losses on the others by selling about a half million. That's a lot for most artists, but when Eddie got going later, RCA was disappointed if that's all he sold. Eddie bought his mother a house on Roosevelt Boulevard in Philadelphia, satisfying one of her lifelong dreams; the house had four bathrooms. Everything was beginning to move beautifully and prosperously for Eddie. Too good, in fact.

Eddie became Private Eddie. He was drafted; underwent basic training with the tank corps at Ft. Hood, then, fresh and youthful-looking in his uniform, he was shipped to the U.S. Army band as soloist. Eddie went on radio or TV and helped with recruiting, with blood drives, bond drives, or any other drives that were handy. He was given a little troupe, and when we ran into him in those days he was always just off to Germany, Alaska, Japan, or Korea; or maybe merely going back to Washington to sing at an official function there.

Instead of finding the Army a place for the burial of his

career, as a few others did, Eddie found that he was only hurt financially. He couldn't be working in theaters or on commercial TV shows of his own, reaping big dough, but he was being heard and he was being well-publicized.

He became a sort of Army symbol, and most people probably thought the Army had done wisely in assigning him to this, rather than less romantic posts and duties.

In a forty-six-day visit to Korea, he sang to more than 100,-000 GIs, and at the Ernie Pyle Theater, in Tokyo, he broke the all-time attendance record held previously by Danny Kaye.

His record sales boomed. "Turn Back the Hands of Time" sold 400,000; "Any Time," recorded in November, 1951 (he was Private Eddie Fisher, *First Class*, about this time), shot up close to the million mark quickly, and hasn't stopped selling yet. It's likely to hit 1,500,000 before it quits. "How Do You Speak to An Angel?" was another of his hits while he was in uniform.

The Fisher legend has it that he first met Debbie Reynolds at Walter Reed Hospital in 1951 when both were there entertaining patients.

"How do you do, Private Fisher?" Debbie said.

"How do you do, Miss Reynolds?" Eddie replied.

Supposedly that's all that happened at the time.

I say "supposedly"; Eddie's always had an eye for beauty, and it's unlikely that he'd let the matter drop there. Still, even by April 10, 1953, when he was discharged from the Army, we gossip columnists didn't have any wind of an Eddie-Debbie romance.

With his release by the Army, Eddie, at twenty-four, began his new career in earnest. He'd just recorded "I'm Walking Behind You," another million-record hit, and on the very day he was discharged, he started a $7,500-a-week engagement at the Paramount Theater. The papers pointed out that he'd worked there once before, leading a community sing at intermissions, and that his pay had been much different.

Seventy-five dollars a week, in fact.

When the Eddie and Debbie romance first blossomed, there

were skeptics who said—even in print—that it was a "publicity gimmick."

Among those who thought so were the Fisher fans who'd strewn flowers in his path when he opened at the Paramount. These young girls couldn't imagine Eddie caring for anybody but them; they couldn't bear the thought.

But as the months went by in 1955 and the marriage didn't take place, there were adults who wondered. After all, movie companies had hitched a star to a star for publicity purposes hundreds of times.

I was one of the many newspapermen who tried to find out the score from Eddie.

One afternoon I went around to the Fisher suite at the Essex House to have a "frank talk" with him. Debbie was in California then. The marriage had been postponed. It looked to be off.

"There's a problem," Eddie admitted.

Well, that was frank, all right. But it was also just about all he'd say about it.

In mid-September, Debbie came to New York, spent most of her time with Eddie, and caused an upsurge in the marriage talk. On the night of September 25—it was a Sunday—I discovered that Debbie's mother, Mrs. Raymond Reynolds, of Burbank, Calif., had sneaked into New York and was having dinner at La Vie, a night club in which Milton Blackstone was interested. Mrs. Reynolds was having dinner with some employees of the Blackstone office.

Well, this did look like a wedding, for sure!

"I suppose you're here for the wedding?" I said.

"What wedding?" Mrs. Reynolds hooted. "I'm a Dodger fan—and I'm in New York for the World Series!"

I mentioned the new rumors about a marriage.

"Those two guys have changed their minds four thousand times, and I don't even ask them any more," Mrs. Reynolds went on. "The only place you can get an answer is from The Man Upstairs—because I don't think those two guys know."

Eddie and Debbie were then week-ending at Grossinger's. Mrs. Reynolds insisted that Eddie had invited her and her husband to use his box at the World Series and they had accepted. I showed Mrs. Reynolds some late-edition papers, about midnight, which predicted the marriage the next day, and Mrs. Reynolds first said, "Isn't that ridiculous?" Then she added, "I'm going to call up those two guys and find out."

Next forenoon she phoned me to say she'd talked to Debbie at Grossinger's and that the wedding was on for seven o'clock that night.

And she also confessed that she'd known it was going to take place during the week, "if those two guys didn't change their minds," but hadn't been sure just when. It also developed that Eddie had told Eddie Cantor on Saturday afternoon that the marriage was to be held within a few hours. All this is to show that there was considerable "uncertain certainty" about this event right up to the time it really took place.

Music was provided by a trio—known in the business as a "combo"—when Debbie entered on her father's arm at the wedding, in the home of Mrs. Elaine Grossinger Etess at Grossinger's. The trio played "Moonlight and Roses" and then switched to the Wedding March from Lohengrin at Debbie's request.

They promised to "love, honor and keep" each other; the word *obey* being eliminated.

A double-ring ceremony was performed by Sullivan County Judge Cook.

It took place on Yom Kippur week-end, and could not be held until after the end of Yom Kippur, which was about 7 P.M. It was set for eight, but delayed another hour so that Eddie's mother might arrive from Philadelphia.

Mary Frances Reynolds, twenty-three, wore a white lace ballerina-length dress with full skirt, trimmed with velvet.

Edwin Jack Fisher, twenty-six, wore a dark business suit.

Eddie kissed Debbie with vast enthusiasm after the ceremony and they vowed to have six children. Next day they went to Washington to spend part of their short honeymoon at a Coca-Cola bottlers' convention.

The first of the promised six children arrived October 21, 1956. A beautiful baby girl whom they named Carrie Frances. Both hope the next will be a boy.

Eddie's marriage to Coca-Cola, NBC, and RCA took place long before his wedding with Debbie. He grew gradually but steadily in stature as a performer until finally in December, 1955, NBC let it be known that it wanted to sign him to a "lifetime"—or—fifteen-year contract. Somebody pointed out that in Eddie's case, at the end of a "lifetime"—or fifteen years —he would only be forty-two!

By now Eddie, although still a boy, is Big Business.

Just the handling of his fan mail and autographed pictures costs him a small fortune. But mostly he sings and rehearses singing.

"Eddie's a guy that lives singing," a friend explained.

"He sings practically all the time. He'll sing any time and any place with almost any excuse. The guy he loves to emulate is Al Jolson, who would go on stage at the Winter Garden and sing for hours."

Eddie employs Willard Higgins, formerly with Milton Berle, as his valet. Eddie's enthusiastic about clothes, and if he sees a sports jacket he likes, he may buy it in several different shades.

Not only that, but if a friend admires a cashmere jacket, Eddie's likely to go to his clothes closet and present him with one.

During Eddie's rise, he's shown a remarkable loyalty to boyhood friends, quite as Frank Sinatra did.

Joey Forman and Bernie Rich have been helped along in the acting business by Eddie. Eddie usually has them at his table at an important dinner or opening if it's possible. When he's off to the Coast, they're likely to be along, and Bernie Rich may be driving one of his cars. Eddie enjoys having these old Philadelphia buddies around. He can relax with them. They're his age.

Barney Ross, the ex-champion, has been on the payroll of the "organization"—this being the loose term for the Fisher-Blackstone partnership arrangement. The veteran composer, Harry Akst, was with Eddie constantly until his illness, and now is in semi-retirement. Axel Stordahl has done TV-show conducting for Eddie. Eddie and Debbie are good friends of

"Ax" and his wife, June Hutton, and they're frequently together.

Eddie has always been generous about sharing credit for his success with those he's worked with; for example, he lets no one praise his string of hit records without reminding them of the "great Hugo Winterhalter."

Nobody can quite state positively what arrangement Eddie has with the man who has worked so hard to make him successful, Milton Blackstone. But it's apparent that it isn't just an artist-agent arrangement.

And Blackstone sure is entitled to a chunk of Eddie's prosperity, for there are people who can recall when he was around town saying, almost apologetically, "I wish you'd listen to a young singer. He doesn't have any reputation yet, but I have a feeling that some day you might hear a lot about him. His name is Eddie Fisher. . . ."

Eddie's matured now—he might even smoke a cigar in private. And now that he's teamed up in a weekly alternate-star arrangement with George Gobel, he's showing his poise, personality and humor—in the Sinatra manner. Still, it's his singing that sells Eddie.

A Tin Pan Alley friend of mine summed up Eddie thusly:

"He may not have the greatest voice—but Eddie Fisher does have the greatest tonsils."

He referred to Eddie's power and endurance—which should keep him singing through a couple of "lifetime" contracts.